YOUR ELITE ENERGY

Your Elite Energy

A Blueprint to Break Free from Burnout and Restore Your Vitality

Bree Bacon

MANUSCRIPTS
PRESS

The manufacturer's authorized representative in the EU for product safety is:
Authorised Rep Compliance Ltd, 71 Lower Baggot Street,
Dublin D02 P593 Ireland
(www.arccompliance.com)

YOUR ELITE ENERGY
A Blueprint to Break Free from Burnout and Restore Your Vitality

ISBN
979-8-88926-391-3 *Paperback*
979-8-88926-392-0 *Hardcover*
979-8-88926-390-6 *eBook*

For Neil and Eliana,
my loves, always and forever.

CONTENTS

———

INTRODUCTION

DID I MISS A CLASS?

"Burnout is what happens when you try
to avoid being human for too long."

—MICHAEL GUNGOR

In December 2021, I stepped back into the fast-paced world of corporate leadership, only to discover the hardest part was not the work. It was staying sane.

As a new mom, I was juggling the whirlwind of motherhood while trying to prove myself in a demanding, high-pressure role. I was eager to succeed in both arenas, doing right by my team and excelling as a new mom to my precious baby girl. I threw myself into both responsibilities with everything I had, 110 percent to my career and 110 percent to my daughter. At first, it seemed to work. I was juggling it all.

Until the panic attacks started. Sleepless nights piled up, and what began as simple exhaustion quickly turned into something far more suffocating. I was not just tired anymore. I was completely overwhelmed, trapped in a cycle of anxiety that made it feel impossible to keep up.

I reached out to doctors, experts, and therapists, desperate for answers. I knew I was not the only working parent juggling a demanding career alongside the stresses of family life. Yet why did it feel like everyone else was managing it better? What was I missing? What was I doing wrong?

I was flooded with advice, but none of it seemed to make a difference. In fact, it only added to the chaos. The endless suggestions were overwhelming, and I could not keep track of what I was supposed to do, why I was doing it, or how it was supposed to help. Worst of all, whose advice was actually right?

Meanwhile, I felt like I was falling short in every direction, letting down my team, my leaders, my daughter, and even my husband. The guilt was suffocating, and the anxiety kept spiraling.

Finally, I hit a breaking point. For someone who hates the idea of "failing," it was a tough decision: I stepped down from my leadership role. I had to face the uncomfortable truth that I could not do it all; that I was human. I needed to prioritize my health and my family. I was completely burned out.

Unfortunately, my experience with burnout is far from unique. According to Deloitte, nearly 70 percent of executives consider quitting due to concerns about their well-being.[1]

Microsoft's *Work Trend Index* reports over 50 percent of managers feel burned out, while Mercer's *Global Talent Trends* takes it even further, stating over 80 percent of employees feel at risk of burnout.[2]

What exactly is burnout?

According to the World Health Organization (WHO), burnout stems from chronic workplace stress that has not been properly managed. It manifests in three key ways: a sense of energy depletion or exhaustion, a growing mental distance from one's work, or a diminished sense of personal accomplishment or capability in completing tasks.[3]

Why is burnout so dangerous?

First and foremost, it is devastating for the individual. A 2015 study by Harvard and Stanford professors found that burnout costs up to $190 billion each year in health care expenses, stemming from issues like mental illness, anxiety, and serious physical conditions such as heart disease. Worse yet, work-related stress is linked to at least 120,000 deaths annually—people working themselves to death.[4]

Burnout is not just a personal issue; it is a serious problem for businesses and organizations too. Extensive research and real-world case studies consistently demonstrate a clear link between employee well-being and overall performance. Simply put, healthy employees are far more likely to produce high-quality work than those weighed down by burnout or stress. The cost of neglecting well-being is far greater than the investment in ensuring it.

The bottom line is that burnout is a widespread issue that affects everyone, from individuals to employers, and ultimately threatens the viability of any project, business, or organization.

We have established the problem, but how do we change it?

As a leader with training from top-tier universities and corporate development programs, I could not help but feel like I had missed a critical class when I went through my own burnout experience. We live in a culture that celebrates working harder, longer hours, and being "always on" in the name of productivity. The message is clear: do more, achieve more, and push yourself to the limit.

Here is what we fail to recognize: energy—the very capacity to do work—is not infinite. It needs to be nurtured, protected, and replenished. No matter how many skills we acquire or how many hours we put in, if we do not learn how to safeguard our energy, we will burnout. In our productivity-driven culture, we have overlooked something fundamental: we must learn how to cultivate and preserve the energy required for sustainable, fulfilling, and high-impact work.

This is where *Your Elite Energy* comes in.

In physics, *energy* stands for the capacity to do work, and *elite*, as an adjective, denotes the best, the choicest, the most effective.[5] Together, *Your Elite Energy* represents your personal best capacity.

Your Elite Energy comes from my own experience recovering from burnout. I have taken what can feel like an overwhelming amount of information and distilled it into a practical, easy-to-understand visual framework. This framework is inspired by Newton's pendulum, a device that in physics illustrates the principle of the conservation of energy.[6]

In this book, I will guide you through the process of defining your *Elite Energy* system. We will begin by helping you establish a strong foundation built on your personal **Values & Beliefs**. From there, we will explore core wellness practices that nurture your **Mind**, **Body**, and **Heart**—your mental, physical, and relational health. Finally, we will tackle how to **Rest**, when to **Reach**, and how all these elements interconnect to optimize your overall well-being, combat burnout, and maximize your best capacity.

Your Elite Energy offers a much-needed framework for individuals, teams, and organizations to define, cultivate, and protect their energy. At a time when burnout rates are skyrocketing, this system is more essential than ever. It empowers both individuals and organizations to harness their energy effectively, creating a culture of sustainable capacity and well-being in an increasingly demanding world.

Whether you are an individual contributor or a leader of large teams, this book is for you. By the end, you will have your personal system for fighting burnout—reducing your stress, improving your confidence, and maximizing your personal best capacity.

Get ready: You are about to define your *Elite Energy* system.

PART I

HOW DID WE GET HERE?

CHAPTER 1

CRASH AND BURN

———

"When you're focusing only on the economic bottom line, you're losing sight of the people who are actually generating what's going to be that bottom line."

—CHRISTINA MASLACH

By the summer of 2022, I hit rock bottom, and I did it in the most dramatic way possible. It was not just exhaustion or stress. I found myself in the emergency room, struggling to breathe, my heart racing so violently that I genuinely feared it might give out. Physically, I felt a loss of control. I thought I might pass out, or worse, die. Panic was consuming me to the point that I could not sleep or even speak coherently. I needed medical intervention.

This was no sudden breakdown. It was the breaking point of a slow, relentless burn that had been smoldering for months; a toxic mix of anxiety, grief, and the weight of endless demands, both personal and professional, that I had tried to juggle and hold together.

The truth is, I was not just managing a demanding career. I was fighting a battle no one could see—a quiet, unrelenting one with postpartum anxiety, a shadow cast by my long and painful journey to motherhood. Eliana, my daughter, is my miracle, but that miracle was preceded by a long road of loss and grief. My husband, Neil, and I endured years of miscarriages, each one shattering our hopes of the family we dreamed of building.

The word "miscarriage" is almost unbearable to me. It feels so cold, so detached. It does not even begin to convey the depth of the bond you form with the child you have lost. You hear their heartbeat, you watch them grow. It is not just an embryo or fetus you are seeing, it is your child. Their presence is felt. You love them. Then, just like that, they are gone. No time to grieve. No real support. Just that single word—"miscarriage"—makes it sound like something small, something easy to move past, like it is just a temporary setback. For Neil and myself, it was not "just" a miscarriage. We lost five children before Eliana. I knew their due dates. I had dreams for each of them. They were real. They were ours, and we lost them.

When Eliana finally arrived, I cherished every moment. Even in that joy, I felt fear: fear of losing her, of sudden infant death syndrome (SIDS), of accidents, of not doing enough to protect her. I could not sleep. I would stare at her video monitor and watch for the slightest rise and fall of her chest, just to make sure she was still breathing. If I let myself relax for even a second, anxiety would flood in, convincing me that something would happen, and it would be my fault. It would be because I did not try hard enough to keep her safe.

At the same time, I was determined to give my new business team everything I had. After sixteen weeks of maternity leave (side note: not nearly enough time after having a child), I returned to the relentless pace of Corporate America. By nature, I am a highly accountable person. Before becoming a parent, I worked hard, burning the midnight oil and pushing myself to exceed expectations. Instead of acknowledging I was in a completely different season of life, I jumped right back in, convinced that I could do it all; that I needed to do it all.

The team I was brought in to lead was in the midst of a challenging transition. The newly formed health services company had recently merged several acquisitions, each with its own distinct culture and history, and now they were all trying to operate under one umbrella. This created a lot of anxiety, uncertainty, and clashes between different ways of working. Within my first few months, the leader who had hired me stepped down, and I found myself reporting to a new boss who was at odds with several other executives.

To make matters even more complicated, we were just emerging from the COVID-19 pandemic, and the company had a major event scheduled for May. A premium client gathering meant to unite all these newly merged companies under a single, cohesive vision. About six weeks into my new role, I was told the company had decided I should take the lead on the event, less than three months before it was set to take place. They had a venue but no client list. No invitations had been sent, no theme had been decided, no schedule had been set, and the budget was wildly unrealistic. To top it all off, the executive team had a lot of differing and conflicting opinions.

The pressure quickly became overwhelming. My first visit to the emergency room happened when the executive team could not come to a consensus on the budget with deadlines passing. It was my first experience with an extreme panic attack. At that point, I was ready to step down, but to their credit the leadership team rallied around me, offering their support to keep me going. I do not like to let things fail, and in hindsight, maybe I should have taken a step back. Instead, I pushed through, rallied the team, and burned the midnight oil to get everyone aligned. Somehow, the team pulled off the event and exceeded everyone's expectations.

At that point, I should have taken a step back to recover, but I didn't. A week later, I received a call from human resources. They informed me that they needed to place a large team under my leadership, and I would report to both the chief sales officer and the chief marketing officer while the company worked out its long-term structure. I knew I should have said no, yet I agreed.

Then came the summer of 2022. What I have not told you yet is that my husband and I found out we were unexpectedly pregnant. Even though it was not planned, I was thrilled, hoping that my body had finally figured out how to carry a baby to full term and that we would be able to add to our family. Unfortunately, we lost our child again, our sixth miscarriage.

The loss sent me over the edge, landing me back in the hospital. I realized I needed to step down from my leadership role so I could focus on my health and my family.

I was beyond burned out. I had completely crashed and burned.

Looking back, I realize I should have shown myself way more compassion. I should have listened to my body sooner, set clear boundaries, and taken time to care for myself. In that season, I thought I had to do it all. I convinced myself I was strong enough to push through, to keep giving, until there was nothing left. Then, I collapsed.

BURNOUT: A SLOW EROSION OF YOUR SPIRIT

Burnout is not a one-time event. It is a gradual, often invisible process that wears you down over time. Looking back at my own journey, I see how the constant juggling of work pressures, personal loss, and parenting struggles slowly drained me. Because it happened so incrementally, it was hard to pinpoint exactly when things started to unravel.

Christina Maslach and Michael Leiter, in their book *The Burnout Challenge*, describe this experience powerfully:

> The short-term strategy of self-sacrifice and speed has become the long-term operating model for many businesses. As one consultant put it, "Everyone's job is now an extreme job." But running at a sprint pace cannot be sustained over a long period; it leads to debilitating

consequences such as ongoing stress experiences, physical exhaustion, sleep deprivation, poor job performance, and disruptions of personal and family life.[1]

What is crucial to understand is that "work" is not just what you do to earn a paycheck. It encompasses everything you carry, both professionally and personally. When the pressures of your job, family, and emotional stress accumulate over time with no adequate balance of resources, support, or self-care to counteract them, burnout becomes almost inevitable.

I hope for your sake that you never reach the point of total collapse that I did. If you are on the path toward burnout, you might start noticing some of these signs creeping in.

1. **You are exhausted.** You feel physically and emotionally drained. It may be hard to muster up the energy to complete even simple tasks. The weight of your responsibilities may overwhelm you. You may be constantly tired, worn out, or feel like you have nothing left to give. This sense of fatigue can make it difficult to concentrate, stay motivated, or feel engaged in activities you once enjoyed. The sheer volume or complexity of tasks in front of you may seem insurmountable, causing you to feel incapable of managing them.

2. **You feel disengaged.** Where you once felt passion, you now may find it difficult to concentrate or care

about your tasks. You may lack interest in work-related activities, feel disconnected from colleagues or clients, or begin to experience a general sense of apathy toward work. This may even escalate to negative attitudes, thoughts, or beliefs about your job or your workplace. You may become increasingly critical, frustrated, or skeptical about your work, coworkers, supervisors, or the organization as a whole.

3. **You lack confidence.** You doubt your own competence and effectiveness in handling your responsibilities. Areas where you previously felt competent, you now doubt your skills, knowledge, or abilities. You may second-guess your decisions or constantly worry about making mistakes. You may feel like you are not deserving, attributing your past successes to luck or good fortune rather than your abilities, achievements, and hard work.

Recognize you do not have to experience all the symptoms to be considered either burned out or on the path to it. For example, you might feel emotionally drained and detached from your work but still have confidence in your abilities. You might be physically exhausted and question your skills but not experience the deep cynicism or distance from your job that some people do.

In my own experience, I was overwhelmed by exhaustion and a lack of confidence in myself, but I never distanced myself mentally or became cynical. If anything, I cared too much. I poured everything into my work and my family, trying to be everything to everyone until I was completely spent.

REFLECT, PROCESS, APPLY

Your turn: Are you burning out? Many tools designed to assess burnout are available, the most widely used instrument being the Maslach Burnout Inventory (MBI), created by Christina Maslach and Susan E. Jackson in 1981.[2] While these assessments are valuable resources, I would like to take a different approach and guide you through an *energy* assessment.

As we discussed earlier, in physics, energy stands for the capacity to do work.[3] Let's take a moment to check in on your current energy levels. Taking stock of your energy can give us insight into whether burnout is beginning to creep in or if you still feel aligned and balanced in managing your responsibilities.

A quick note: This is not a diagnostic tool but rather self-assessment questions I have created to help you reflect on the three areas discussed above—exhaustion, disengagement, and lack of confidence. If you find yourself concerned or uncertain, I highly recommend seeking support from a health care professional, counselor, or therapist. These experts can provide personalized guidance and help you explore your specific situation in more depth.

Your Energy Self-Assessment

Full of Vitality ←————————————→ **Exhausted**

Do you feel physically and emotionally drained?

never	*almost never*	*sometimes*	*often*	*always*

0 1 2 3 4 5 6 7 8 9 1 0

Do you struggle to complete tasks at work or home?

never	*almost never*	*sometimes*	*often*	*always*

0 1 2 3 4 5 6 7 8 9 1 0

How frequently do you feel tired, worn out, or overwhelmed by your responsibilities?

never	*almost never*	*sometimes*	*often*	*always*

0 1 2 3 4 5 6 7 8 9 1 0

Motivated ←————————————→ **Disengaged**

Do you dread going to work?

never	*almost never*	*sometimes*	*often*	*always*

0 1 2 3 4 5 6 7 8 9 1 0

Do you find it hard to care about or feel invested in your job tasks?

never	*almost never*	*sometimes*	*often*	*always*

0 1 2 3 4 5 6 7 8 9 1 0

How often does work frustrate you?

never   almost never   sometimes   often   always

0   1   2   3   4   5   6   7   8   9   1 0

Do you think negatively about your coworkers, supervisors, or organization?

never   almost never   sometimes   often   always

0   1   2   3   4   5   6   7   8   9   1 0

Confident ←——————————→ **Full of Doubt**

Do you doubt your ability to complete tasks effectively or meet work-related goals?

never   almost never   sometimes   often   always

0   1   2   3   4   5   6   7   8   9   1 0

Do you question your skills and abilities?

never   almost never   sometimes   often   always

0   1   2   3   4   5   6   7   8   9   1 0

Do you second-guess your decisions or worry about making mistakes?

never   almost never   sometimes   often   always

0   1   2   3   4   5   6   7   8   9   1 0

Your Total Score: _____

0–10: I am thriving (*Elite Energy*)
11–40: I am hanging in there but could be better (Okay Energy)
41–70: I am burning out (Lack of Energy)
71–100: I am burned out (Limited to No Energy)

No matter where you currently stand with your energy levels, by the end of our journey together, you will have a system in place to protect and maximize your personal *Elite Energy*.

However, before we discuss the *Elite Energy* framework, let's first take a moment to explore why burnout is not only harmful to individuals but also detrimental to organizations, impacting not just their bottom line but their ability to accomplish their mission.

CHAPTER 2

I AM NOT ALONE

———

"Take care of your employees, and they will take care of your business. It's as simple as that."

—RICHARD BRANSON

Unfortunately, my struggle with burnout is far from unique. We have already looked at statistics from Deloitte, Microsoft, and Mercer, but if you need further evidence, plenty more is out there.

Data collected by Gallup reveals that 35 percent of managers of people report being burned out "very often" or "always."[1] The American Psychological Association's 2023 *Work in America* survey paints an even somber picture: "77 percent of workers reported experiencing work-related stress in the past month."[2] Fifty-seven percent indicated they have felt the effects of workplace burnout, including emotional exhaustion, a desire to quit, reduced productivity, irritability or anger toward coworkers and customers, and a sense of ineffectiveness.[3]

Mindy Shoss, a professor of psychology at the University of Central Florida and associate editor for the *Journal of Occupational Health Psychology*, offers some insight into this alarming trend. She explains, "There are many potential causes of burnout in today's workplaces— excessive workloads, low levels of support, having little say or control over workplace matters, lack of recognition or rewards for one's efforts, and interpersonally toxic and unfair work environments [...] it's no surprise that burnout is on the rise in many workplaces."[4]

The data is clear: Burnout is becoming more widespread, and it is undermining both individual well-being and organizational success.

THE PERSONAL CONSEQUENCES OF BURNOUT

Considering the statistics, it is highly likely that at some point in your career you will experience or already are facing symptoms of burnout. Whether you are currently struggling with it or heading toward it, burnout can have profound effects on your personal well-being. In today's fast-paced, high-pressure work environment, constant demands for productivity and availability can leave you feeling mentally, physically, and emotionally drained. It can become so ingrained in your routine that it feels "normal," as though it is simply part of the job. That it is just a part of being a working adult. However, it is crucial to recognize that burnout can have severe, long-lasting consequences on your health, relationships, and overall quality of life.

MENTAL IMPACTS

In a world that constantly demands more, it is easy to fall into the trap of believing your brain can operate at full capacity without rest. However, the reality is that the human brain is not built for nonstop work. Chronic stress from overwork can have severe consequences on your cognitive and mental health.

Llewellyn E. van Zyl, a professor of positive psychology at North-West University, explains that prolonged exposure to work-related stress causes excessive levels of cortisol, a stress hormone. This not only depletes your mental energy but can physically alter the structure of your brain, causing it to "short-circuit and shrink." This brain strain results in a significant decline in cognitive abilities, including memory loss, difficulty focusing, and reduced verbal skills. Multitasking becomes harder, impulse control weakens, and your ability to process and learn new information diminishes.[5]

Burnout does not just affect your ability to think clearly, it can also lead to serious mental health issues. A 2017 study published in *PLoS ONE* reviewed decades of research and found a strong link between job burnout and various mental health issues. These include increased symptoms of depression, a higher reliance on psychotropic medications and antidepressants, and even hospitalization for mental disorders. The chronic stress and emotional exhaustion that come with burnout can exacerbate existing mental health conditions or trigger new ones, making it a significant risk to both your psychological well-being and your overall mental health.[6]

As Llewellyn further points out, "Stress fries your brain's control circuits, making you more scatterbrained, impulsive, and mentally fuzzy. [...] Burnout thus steals much more than just your energy and drive. It robs you of your intelligence."[7]

PHYSICAL IMPACTS

Burnout not only takes a toll on your mental health, it can also severely affect your physical health. The chronic stress associated with burnout can lead to a range of serious physical issues, many of which develop slowly but have long-term consequences.

Dr. Ian Kronish, an associate director of the Center for Behavioral Cardiovascular Health at Columbia University, emphasizes that many people only realize the physical cost of stress after experiencing a major health event, such as a heart attack or stroke. In hindsight, they often recognize that stress played a significant role, but rarely do they connect the dots before the damage occurs. As he notes, "They don't think beforehand that they'd better take care of that stress for their health."[8]

The 2017 study in *PLoS ONE* found that job burnout is associated with a wide range of physical health issues, including high cholesterol, type 2 diabetes, coronary heart disease, musculoskeletal pain, and various gastrointestinal and respiratory problems. The study also pointed to an increased risk of severe fatigue, headaches, and even premature death, particularly among individuals under the age of forty-five.[9] As already mentioned in our introduction, a 2015 study by researchers from Harvard and Stanford found that work-related stress contributes to at least 120,000 deaths each year, underscoring just how serious burnout can be.[10]

In addition to these direct health effects, burnout can lead to unhealthy coping behaviors that worsen the physical toll. Dr. Kronish points out that burnout often drives people to engage in habits like smoking, drinking more alcohol, and poor sleep—all of which have significant biological consequences.[11] The combination of stress and these detrimental behaviors compounds the risks, accelerating the negative impact burnout has on your body and overall well-being.

RELATIONAL IMPACTS

Burnout can also take a significant toll on your social and relational health. When you are burned out, it becomes much harder to manage your emotions, leading to increased irritability, frustration, and emotional exhaustion. This can have serious consequences for both your personal and professional relationships.

Research conducted by scientists at the Karolinska Institutet in Sweden found that burnout can alter brain function in ways that make it harder to regulate emotions. The study compared two groups: One group consisted of individuals who had worked in high-stress conditions for several years, often putting in sixty to seventy hours per week, while the second group was made up of healthy individuals with no history of chronic stress. The results showed significant emotional differences between the two groups, with those experiencing burnout reporting greater difficulty in managing negative emotions. Brain scans revealed a key factor: The amygdala, the part of the brain responsible for processing emotions like fear and aggression, was enlarged in the burnout group. Additionally, there were weaker connections between the amygdala and brain regions involved in emotion regulation. The more stressed the individuals felt, the weaker the connection between these areas, which may explain the heightened emotional sensitivity that often accompanies burnout.[12]

This heightened emotional sensitivity can make it easy to feel frustrated or irritated over minor issues, leading to strain in both work and personal relationships, potentially resulting in conflicts and social withdrawal. It also makes it easier to overreact to small stressors, leading to conflicts at work and in your personal life. Relationships, which are essential for providing emotional support and resilience, can suffer as a result.

Nicole McNichols, an associate teaching professor in psychology at the University of Washington, explains the irony: "The support that comes from a healthy relationship fuels our energy and resilience. It helps us cope with other life stressors. Yet even the best relationships suffer when one or both partners feel burnt out."[13] Burnout can leave you too drained to invest in the very relationships that could help you recover, resulting in social withdrawal and isolation.

For you as an individual, the research is clear: Protecting and investing in your energy is essential for both your well-being; your mental, physical and relational health; and your long-term success. Burnout does not just impact your personal health. It can have lasting consequences on your ability to work and make a meaningful impact.

Before we discuss solutions for combating burnout (spoiler alert: It involves your *Elite Energy* system), let's take a step back and recognize that burnout is not just a personal issue; it also poses a significant risk to organizations.

BURNOUT'S PRICE TAG: THE IMPACT ON THE BOTTOM LINE

For some, it is intuitive that burnout negatively impacts business. However, for those raised in a "work hard, play hard" environment, this concept can feel counterintuitive to achieving results. Many believe that pushing harder, increasing hours, and applying more pressure on themselves and their team will drive higher productivity and better outcomes.

I think back to my days as an investment banker (a long, long time ago). Bankers would swap stories about closing deals while skiing down mountains on "vacation" or working nonstop for days, taking only a few days off in their entire careers, weekends included. We often stayed up until 1:00 or 2:00 a.m. working on client presentations, only to wake back up at 6:00 or 7:00 a.m. to head back into the grind. I remember once being so sleep-deprived that while doing my hair in the morning I made a mistake and instinctively thought, *Control Z*—like I could just undo it the way you can on a computer. I got frustrated when the computer shortcut did not work in real life and couldn't magically fix my hair. Weekends were no different. If you weren't in the office, it was considered odd. One colleague had a cot under his desk for quick naps, while another kept a laundry basket with his dirty clothes at his workstation because he was there so long.

For those who have built their careers in a similar culture, this section is for you. We have already explored the real mental, physical, and social toll burnout takes on your health and, if you are a leader, the well-being of your team. Now, let's examine another critical angle: why employee burnout is not just harmful to well-being but also undermines the bottom line.

I want to make it clear that investing in well-being goes far beyond simply boosting profits. Leaders and employers do have a deeper responsibility to care for those who contribute to their mission. However, it is also crucial to recognize the financial consequences of burnout. Many still believe that productivity and well-being are in conflict, but in reality, investing in well-being is the key to unlocking true capacity and sustainable success.

For organizations, the costs of burnout are steep. From decreased productivity and engagement to higher rates of absenteeism and turnover, burnout directly impacts a company's efficiency and bottom line. If you are a leader or investor, the long-term effects on team morale and performance can jeopardize growth and profitability.

A comprehensive study published in *Population Health Management* in 2013 aimed to examine the connection between employee well-being and key factors affecting an organization's profits. The researchers focused on three critical areas: health care outcomes (such as total health care expenditures, emergency room visits, and hospitalizations); productivity outcomes (including unscheduled absenteeism, short-term disability leave, presenteeism, and job performance ratings); and retention outcomes (like intention to stay, voluntary turnover, and involuntary turnover).[14]

The findings were striking. The study concluded that health care costs, lost productivity, and turnover were significant financial burdens for employers. In fact, private employers in the United States were estimated to spend over $500 billion annually on health care costs related to burnout. Additionally, businesses were losing over $200 billion per year due to lost productivity, while turnover, both voluntary and involuntary, was impacting earnings by anywhere from 12 to 40 percent.[15]

While this study is now over a decade old, its categories still provide a solid framework for understanding the economic toll of burnout on organizations. Let's explore some updated statistics that further highlight the financial consequences burnout continues to have on companies.

HEALTH CARE COSTS

As we have discussed, burnout can take a serious toll on an individual's health. It is not just about feeling stressed. It can lead to physical conditions such as diabetes, heart disease, and respiratory problems. Mental health is equally impacted, with burnout contributing to conditions such as depression, anxiety, and reliance on psychotropic and antidepressant medications. In fact, it is estimated that 60 to 80 percent of primary health care visits have a stress-related component.[16]

These health issues require ongoing medical attention, from doctor visits and medications to potential hospitalizations. As you can imagine, this means higher health care utilization over time, which translates to rising costs. If your company offers health insurance as a benefit to its employees (as over 50 percent of companies in the United States do), these increasing health care expenses will directly hit your bottom line.[17]

Researchers have found the health care expenditures of workers who report high levels of stress are "46 percent greater than workers with low levels of stress."[18] In the 2013 *Population Health Management* study, the original estimate of over $500 billion in health care costs was sourced from the KFF, which calculated that private employers in the United States were responsible for roughly 20 percent of all health care expenditures in the country.[19] Back in 2010, the United States spent $2.6 trillion on health care, averaging $8,402 per person.[20] Fast forward to the latest estimates in 2023, United States health care spending has ballooned to $4.9 trillion, or $14,570 per person, with private employers now contributing 18 percent of that total, over $880 billion.[21]

The rise in health care costs is not just a United States issue. WTW, a global advisory firm, conducted the 2024 Global Medical Trends Survey tracking medical costs across 266 insurers in sixty-six countries. The findings were illuminating: The annual global increases in medical rates jumped from 7.4 percent in 2022 to a record high of 10.7 percent in 2023, with over half of insurers expecting higher or significantly higher medical trends over the next three years.[22]

If you are responsible for the financial well-being of your organization, that is a lot of dollars out the door. Ouch.

LOST PRODUCTIVITY

In 2003, the American Productivity Audit conducted a comprehensive study to assess how health conditions, including burnout, impact workplace productivity. The study focused on lost productive time (LPT), which refers to time employees are unable to contribute effectively due to health issues. The results were eye-opening: health-related LPT was costing employers over $200 billion per year.[23]

A decade later, Gallup's State of the American Workplace report added even more insight into the costs of disengaged employees. Gallup found that 70 percent of United States workers are either "'not engaged' or 'actively disengaged' at work, meaning they are emotionally disconnected and less likely" to put forth their best efforts. Gallup estimates these disengaged employees are costing companies between $450 billion to $550 billion annually in lost productivity. The report also reveals that disengaged employees are more likely to "steal from their companies, negatively influence coworkers, miss workdays, and drive customers away," all of which compounds the financial toll on organizations.[24]

Burnout's effects on productivity go beyond disengagement. It also directly impairs an employee's cognitive abilities. Decades of research shows that employees experiencing burnout exhibited significant cognitive deficits, including impaired short-term memory, attention, and decision-making, all of which are essential for daily work tasks. When employees are overwhelmed by stress or exhaustion, their ability to prioritize, stay organized, or maintain focus for extended periods becomes severely compromised. This results in delays, errors, and incomplete work, which only further drain productivity and contributes to a cycle of reduced performance.[25]

Finally, burnout also significantly contributes to increased absenteeism, as employees may need time off to recover from exhaustion or address mental health issues. A 2010 study found that employees experiencing burnout have a 57 percent increased risk of being absent from work for more than two weeks due to illness.[26] Furthermore, the American Psychological Association reports "that 550 million workdays are lost each year due to stress on the job."[27]

In 2017, Gallup updated their previous estimates, revealing that disengaged employees now cost between $483 billion and $605 billion annually in lost productivity.[28]

Double ouch.

EMPLOYEE TURNOVER

High levels of burnout not only reduce productivity but also significantly increase employee turnover. According to MyPerfectResume, one in five workers are so burned out, they consider quitting every day.[29] A 2021 Visier survey found that "89 percent of employees experienced burnout in the past year," and "70 percent of them said they would leave their jobs because of it."[30]

The American Psychological Society emphasizes that employers who fail to provide adequate mental health and well-being support are also hurting their ability to recruit and retain talent. Of all workers, 33 percent said they planned to look for a new job within the next year. "Among those workers who said they are unsatisfied with the mental health and well-being support offered by their employer, that number rose to 57 percent."[31]

Replacing these departed employees can have a significant bottom-line impact for organizations. A 2006 PricewaterhouseCoopers report estimated that employee turnover costs employers 12 to 40 percent of a company's earnings.[32] In 2019, Gallup found that voluntary turnover was costing American businesses a trillion dollars annually.

On a per-employee basis, Gallup estimates that "replacing an individual employee can range anywhere from one-half to two times their annual salary."[33] In 2023, the average rate of voluntary turnover rate was 17.3 percent.[34] If you run a 100-person organization with an average salary of $56,000, you are likely to have seventeen of your employees leave, costing you between $476,000 to $1.9 million annually.

Triple ouch.

The conclusion from these three areas—health care costs, productivity losses, and employee turnover—is clear: Burnout is draining your organization. The dollars lost across these factors can significantly impact your bottom line, affecting both your organization's financial health and long-term success.

REFLECT, PROCESS, APPLY
Your turn: Before continuing, take a moment to reflect. The following questions are meant to help you process and relate the material to your own experiences.

1. Based on the mental, physical, and relational impacts of burnout discussed in this chapter, can you identify moments in your career where you have experienced similar effects? How did burnout manifest in your own life, and how did you manage it?

_____

_____

_____

_____

_____

_____

2. How does the work environment you are currently in
   (or have been in) contribute to stress or burnout? What
   factors in the culture—such as workload, support, or
   recognition—might be influencing your well-being?

_____

_____

_____

_____

_____

_____

3. When was the last time you felt truly energized and
   engaged in your work or personal life? What conditions were in place during that time?

_____

_____

_____

_____

_____

_____

NOW WHAT?

We have established the problem. Burnout is a real and growing issue. It takes a toll on individuals, impacts employers, and damages organizations. The troubling reality is that burnout rates are not slowing down. In fact, they are getting worse.

How do we solve it? Is there a way to approach work and life that can combat burnout rather than just managing its symptoms?

As Jeffrey Pfeffer, author of _Dying for a Paycheck_, powerfully states, "Societies would benefit from movements that resolutely take the importance and sanctity of human life and people's physical and psychological well-being more seriously—not just at life's very, very beginning or at its very, very end, but throughout people's lives, including their lives at work."[35] This quote underscores a crucial truth about burnout: It is not something that just happens to us; it is a result of the choices we make, both as individuals and as organizations. If we do not take control of how we work, rest, and recharge, burnout will continue to take over our lives.

Here is the good news: We have the power to change. We do not have to accept burnout as an inevitable part of the modern work experience. Together, we can start a movement that challenges all of us to take well-being seriously, not just in theory but in practice; one that reshapes how we approach work and well-being, making it sustainable and human-centered.

Let me introduce you to your *Elite Energy* system, the framework to combat burnout and reclaim your vitality, both personally and professionally. It is time to unlock your best capacity.

CHAPTER 3

PROFESSOR PHYSICS

—

"Energy, not time, is the fundamental
currency of high performance."

—JIM LOEHR

After my first miscarriage, I began to experience intense anxiety. I would feel such joy when I found out I was pregnant again, but that joy would quickly turn into dread. As embarrassing as this is, even the simplest things, like going to the bathroom, became loaded with fear. I could not shake the thought that something could be wrong; that my body was somehow betraying me, killing my babies. I was determined to keep trying for a child, but I knew I had to confront this overwhelming fear and these irrational thoughts, or at least learn how to manage them, if I was ever going to move forward.

In search of some professional guidance, I decided to see a therapist for the first time in my life. During our first session, she introduced me to a tool that turned out to be surprisingly effective when anxiety felt overwhelming. It is called the 5-4-3-2-1 technique.[1]

Here is how it works:

- **Sight**: Look around and name five things you can see.
- **Touch**: Describe four things you can feel.
- **Hear**: Identify three distinct sounds you can hear.
- **Smell**: Name two scents you can smell.
- **Taste**: Focus on one thing you can taste.

When your mind starts to spiral, or when anxiety takes over, this exercise helps ground you, shifting your brain from an emotional state back to a more rational one. It encourages you to focus on the present moment and connect with your surroundings through each of your senses. The beauty of this exercise is its simplicity. It provides a structured way to calm your anxious thoughts. This grounding technique does not require special training or complicated steps. I even use it on airplanes during turbulence to calm my nerves.

Having a simple tool I could put into action was a game-changer during moments of anxiety. It gave me something concrete I could do, something I could control. However, when navigating my journey through burnout, I did not have a clear tool or framework to guide me through it.

Instead, I was bombarded with well-meaning advice—*Take a day off, Go for a walk, Try yoga, Read a book*—but none of it felt like it fit together. It all seemed like isolated suggestions that did not address the bigger picture or tackle the root of the burnout. I ended up feeling more scattered, unsure of where to start, and overwhelmed by the sheer number of solutions that did not seem tailored to me.

That is when the *Elite Energy* framework was born. I took everything I learned from my personal struggles with burnout, anxiety, and recovery and turned it into a system—a simple, visual tool that breaks down the essential components needed to manage and maximize your energy in a way that is sustainable, manageable, and, most importantly, effective. Now, whenever I start to feel burnout creeping in, I use this visual framework. I am excited to share it with you!

FIRST, A PHYSICS LESSON

Newton's pendulum, also known as Newton's cradle, is most often recognized as an executive desk decoration.[2]

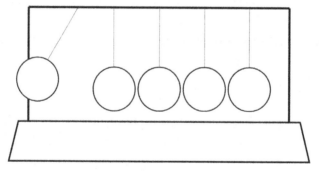

Image #1: Newton's Pendulum (Source: Bree Bacon)

The device typically consists of five identical metal balls suspended from a frame with thin wires and positioned to just barely touch one another. When you pull one of the end balls away from the others and then release it, it hits the core balls in the middle, transmitting its force through to the opposite end where the fifth ball is pushed into the air. Then that ball swings back, repeating the effect in the opposite direction. This creates a rhythm back and forth between the end two balls, taking turns being pushed into the air and striking the middle core balls.

In the world of physics, this device helps demonstrate a few principles, but one in particular I would like to call out is the conservation of energy. The continuous clicking rhythm of the balls demonstrates that energy cannot be created or destroyed, but it can change forms.[3] Newton's pendulum demonstrates it quite well, as it converts the energy from one ball into energy that is transferred down the line of balls and ultimately results in the upward push of the last ball.

The conservation of energy in Newton's pendulum is a great metaphor for our own personal energy. Just as energy in the pendulum is finite, our energy, too, must be protected and invested in ways that align with sustaining our best capacity.

As a reminder, *energy*, in physics, is defined as the capacity to do work.[4] Contrary to the common belief that working harder and longer always leads to success, the truth is that our energy—our capacity—is finite. This is where the concept of "elite" comes in.

Elite, as an adjective, stands for your best.[5] To reach your highest potential—whether for yourself, your family, your team, or your organization—it is essential to focus on maximizing and optimizing the energy you have.

Together, your *Elite Energy* represents your personal *best capacity*.

THE FRAMEWORK

As a tool to demonstrate the conservation of energy, Newton's pendulum serves as a powerful parallel for our own personal energy and a fitting visual framework for understanding and applying your personal *elite* energy, your best capacity.

Let's take a quick tour of the framework.

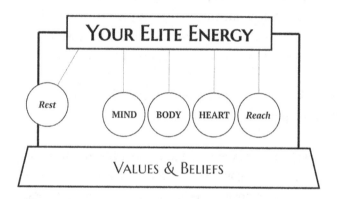

Image 2: Your Elite Energy Framework (source: Bree Bacon)

At the base of our framework is your personal **Values & Beliefs**. These are the foundation of everything you do, the bedrock that keeps you grounded as you navigate challenges and decisions. Everything in the framework builds on this foundation.

Next, we move to what I call the **core**—the three central components of your system: *Mind, Body,* and *Heart.*

- **Mind** represents your mental health and wellness. It is about realizing your abilities, effectively coping with and navigating stress, and producing work that is both impactful and sustainable.

- **Body** represents your physical health and wellness. It is the state in which all your internal and external body systems—organs, muscles, tissues, and cells—are functioning at their best.

- **Heart** represents your relational health and wellness. It is about the quality of your relationships and your ability to connect with others, which are essential for emotional support and motivation.

Finally, we introduce *Rest* and *Reach*—the components that help you maintain balance.

- **Rest** encompasses the regular practices you engage in for relaxation, enjoyment, and recovery. It is about carving out time to unwind, recharge, and celebrate progress. Regular rest is essential to ensuring your energy remains sustainable, helping you avoid burnout.

- **Reach** represents the stretch goals you set for yourself, or challenges that push you to grow, learn, and demonstrate your ability to make an impact. By consistently stretching yourself, you build resilience and expand your capacity to take on new challenges.

As we move into Part II, we will go deeper into each component of the framework and explore how you can apply it to maximize your *Elite Energy*.

HEALTH VERSUS WELLNESS VERSUS WELL-BEING

Before we continue on our journey, I want to clarify how I distinguish between health, wellness, and well-being.

- **Health** refers to your current state of being and any goals for improvement. It is about your condition right now and where you want to go.

- **Wellness** encompasses the actions you take, your regular practices and habits designed to achieve and maintain your desired state of health.

- **Well-being** describes the overall condition of your whole self. It is how all the components of your *Elite Energy* system—*Values & Beliefs, Mind, Body, Heart, Rest,* and *Reach*—work together to support the overall effectiveness of your ecosystem. It is how your wellness practices in each area come together to create a version of you who is not just surviving but truly thriving.

Let's illustrate these terms using the physical aspect of your *Elite Energy* system: your *Body*.

- **Physical health** refers to your current condition and any goals for improvement. For example, if your blood pressure is 140/100, your goal might be to lower it to 120/80. Alternatively, you may aim to maintain a healthy blood pressure of 120/80.

- **Physical wellness** involves the actions and habits you adopt to achieve or maintain that goal. This could include reducing your salt intake, taking daily walks, or managing stress through stretching and breathing exercises.

Together, your physical health and wellness—your current state, goals, and consistent practices—contribute to your overall well-being. These choices impact the care of your whole self and support the overall effectiveness of your *Elite Energy* system, ultimately enhancing your ability to unlock and sustain your best capacity.

YOUR SYSTEM IS AN ECOSYSTEM

While I have broken down the elements of your well-being into distinct categories, our human experience is complex and interconnected. You cannot combat burnout by focusing solely on your physical health while neglecting your mental or relational health. You also cannot keep pushing yourself to constantly reach and challenge yourself without balancing that with rest and recovery (trust me, I have tried).

Additionally, many of the core wellness practices we will discuss in one category impact other areas of your health. For example, research shows that physical exercise releases feel-good chemicals called endorphins in the brain. Even a brisk ten-minute walk can improve mental alertness, boost energy, and elevate your mood, demonstrating how a wellness practice for your *Body* directly affects the health of your *Mind*.[6] Similarly, strong social connections are linked to longer life, reduced stress, and improved heart health, showing how a wellness practice for your *Heart* also supports the health of your *Body*.[7]

We are complex, which is exactly why we focus on defining and investing in your *Elite Energy* system as an ecosystem. An ecosystem is a complex network of interconnected systems, each made up of various processes, activities, and relationships that influence one another.

In the same way, the components of your *Elite Energy* system—*Values & Beliefs, Mind, Body, Heart, Rest,* and *Reach*—interact with and build upon one another to combat burnout and maximize your energy. This system recognizes that every area of your life influences your overall well-being. When one part is out of balance, it can throw off your entire ecosystem, limiting your ability to perform and feel at your best.

You might already be investing in one area of your *Elite Energy* system. Perhaps you are great at working out every morning but struggle to sleep at night due to racing thoughts. Maybe you meditate regularly but struggle with poor eating habits that leave you feeling sluggish. To effectively combat burnout, you cannot focus on just one aspect of your ecosystem. You need to define, invest in, and protect *all* elements of your system.

Experts agree that a holistic approach is essential. Unites States Surgeon General Dr. Vivek Murthy states, "A healthy workforce is the foundation for thriving organizations and healthier communities [...] We have an opportunity and the power to make workplaces engines for mental health and well-being." He goes on to say, "It will require organizations to rethink how they protect workers from harm, foster a sense of connection among workers, show workers that they matter, make space for their lives outside work, and support their growth. It will be worth it, because the benefits will accrue for workers and organizations alike."[8]

You might be thinking, *This sounds great, but I already have too much on my plate. I don't have time to reflect on my ecosystem, or think about my physical and mental health, or figure out how to relax and recharge.*

Many of us respond to the rising demands at work and the stress in our lives by putting in longer hours and taking on more, often at the expense of our well-being. However, as we discussed in the previous chapter, this only leads to declining engagement, higher turnover, increasing levels of distraction, and rising medical costs—not to mention the personal cost to your own well-being, joy, meaning, and happiness.

Defining and investing in your *Elite Energy* system is exactly what will help you become more productive and effective. Yes, you will get more done, be more efficient, and, most importantly, find more joy in the process.

Let's look at some real-life case studies from each area of impact discussed earlier. We will see how focusing on individuals' ecosystems can positively influence productivity, reduce health care costs, lower turnover, and ultimately create a more engaged, fulfilled, and thriving organizational culture.

WACHOVIA BANK: PRODUCTIVITY[9]

In early 2006, Tony Schwartz, CEO and founder of the Energy Project, led a group of 106 employees from Wachovia Bank through an energy management program. This month-long initiative included a four-module curriculum focused on improving physical, emotional, and mental wellness. Participants were also paired with a colleague for additional support between sessions.

Schwartz and his team evaluated the participants' performance against a control group, tracking year-over-year changes in Wachovia's key revenue metrics, which were based on three specific loan types. The results were notable: Participants surpassed the control group by 13 percentage points in the first three months. In terms of one particular metric, revenue from deposits, they outperformed the control group by 20 percentage points. Furthermore, this enhanced performance persisted for a full year after the program concluded.

Beyond the financial improvements, participants were surveyed about the personal impact of the program. Sixty-eight percent reported better relationships with clients and customers, while 71 percent said the program had a noticeable or significant positive effect on their productivity and performance.

KENT STATE UNIVERSITY: MEDICAL COST SAVINGS[10]

Kent State University (KSU) has about six thousand employees across Ohio and New York. After surveys revealed mental health and work-life balance as major staff concerns, they worked to launch new wellness initiatives. The university expanded its Employee Assistance Program (EAP), offering support for stress, anxiety, depression, caregiving, and financial/legal issues. They also introduced workshops to help supervisors identify depression signs and implemented programs like "walk and talks" for employee engagement and physical activity.

Within the first six months, a noticeable rise in EAP usage occurred, with more employees seeking assistance for mental health issues. In the year following the program's introduction, the university saw a decline in medical claims from employees diagnosed with depression, saving almost $5,000 per employee annually, which amounted to over $1 million in total savings.

Beyond the financial benefits, the initiative significantly boosted employee morale. The number of employees who felt their organization genuinely cared about their well-being tripled. As a result of these efforts, KSU was recognized as one of the "Great Colleges to Work For," and the university has had eleven consecutive years of receiving this honor since the program's implementation.

9-1-1 DISPATCHERS: TURNOVER REDUCTION[11]

Emergency dispatchers are highly susceptible to burnout due to the stressful and traumatic nature of their work.

For example, over 40 percent of dispatchers in the Los Angeles Police Department report high levels of burnout. Researchers at University of California, Berkeley believed that improving emotional health through social connections and a sense of value could help reduce this burnout.

To test this, over 500 dispatchers across nine United States cities participated in a six-week intervention. Each week, they received an email featuring a personal story from a dispatcher, as well as encouragement to reflect on and share their own experiences. For example, one email told the story of a dispatcher who had saved a woman's life during a domestic violence situation, with a prompt encouraging peers to share similar impactful experiences. This practice helped build a sense of community, empathy, and support among dispatchers.

At the end of the study, two-thirds of participants wanted the emails to continue, and those who took part reported a decrease in burnout. "One model suggests this intervention could reduce turnover by up to 50 percent," potentially saving cities over $400,000 in recruitment and training costs for a 100-person dispatch team.

This example also makes a strong case for integrating *Elite Energy* practices into the workplace to support emotional well-being and social connectedness. While this particular study focused on emotional health through shared stories, the broader takeaway is that fostering a sense of community and support among employees can have a lasting positive impact on both individual well-being and organizational outcomes (more on that in chapter 12).

WHAT'S NEXT?

Now that you understand the importance of defining and investing in your *Elite Energy* system, it is time to put that knowledge into action. The time you spend nurturing your *Elite Energy* system is time well spent. It will help you be more effective, more satisfied, and ultimately combat burnout. It will unlock your best capacity to do meaningful, impactful, and fulfilling work.

That is exactly what we will focus on for the rest of our time together.

In Part II, we will focus on what you can do as an individual to take control of your personal *Elite Energy* system. Each chapter will break down one key component of the system: your foundational *Values & Beliefs*, your core (*Mind*, *Body*, and *Heart*), and the ways you *Rest* and *Reach*. We will explore what each component means, why it is essential for combating burnout, and how these elements work together to help you optimize your energy.

Then, we will help you identify and commit to the key habits and practices you need to build and sustain your own best capacity and overall well-being. This process will guide you through defining your personal wellness commitments for each component and help you complete your *Elite Energy* worksheet, highlighted below and available to print www.BreeBacon.com.[12]

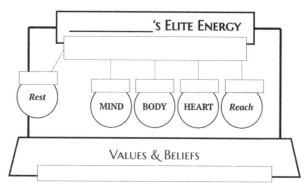

Image 3: Your Elite Energy Worksheet (source: Bree Bacon)

By the end of Part II, you will have defined your number one wellness commitment for each area of your system, giving you a clear roadmap to your *Elite Energy*.

In Part III, once you have defined your individual system, we will focus on how to put those commitments into practice. We will explore creating a rhythm around your commitments, how to leverage the framework when life gets tough, and how to turn your *Elite Energy* into a team sport.

REFLECT, PROCESS, APPLY

Your turn: Before moving on, take a moment to reflect on the ideas we have just explored and think about how they resonate with your own experiences.

1. Do you see your well-being as an interconnected system where your physical, mental, and relational health, your

balance of resting and reaching, influence one another? How have you seen this play out in your own life?

_____

_____

_____

_____

_____

_____

2. Have you ever noticed how improving one area of your life, like physical health, can have a ripple effect on other areas, such as your mental or emotional health? Can you share an example?

_____

_____

_____

_____

_____

_____

3. How do you currently balance the different elements of your well-being, and what areas do you feel could currently use more attention?

_____

_____

_____

_____

_____

_____

FINAL THOUGHTS

As we prepare to define your personal _Elite Energy_ system, I want to leave you with two important reflections.

FIRST, TAKE IT ONE STEP AT A TIME

As we progress through this journey together, please remember that you do not have to make drastic changes all at once. Small shifts can have a powerful impact. In the story of the 9-1-1 dispatchers, for example, something as simple as a weekly email made a big difference in their well-being, energy, and effectiveness. Research by Wharton professor Katherine Milkman affirms that small, manageable steps can help people face challenges, make fresh starts, and adopt healthier habits. These incremental changes can add up to lasting improvements over time.[13]

As we define your *Elite Energy* system, we will start by assessing what you are currently doing in each area—your *Values & Beliefs, Mind, Body, Heart, Rest*, and *Reach*. From there, we will identify what you want to start, stop, and continue doing to maximize your energy. The key is to make one small, meaningful commitment to move forward in each area. These focused steps should make a real difference in your well-being without overwhelming you.

SECOND, MAKE IT PERSONAL

This journey is all about defining a system that works for you. What works for someone else might not be the best fit for you, and that is okay.

In Gretchen Rubin's book *The Happiness Project*, she talks about the importance of embracing what brings you joy, even if it does not align with conventional expectations. Rubin realized that, while she wished she were the type of person who enjoyed high-brow art and the symphony, that was not true to who she was. Instead, she focused on what truly made her happy—like hosting a children's literature book club. By doing so, she was able to align her habits with what genuinely worked for her.[14]

I will share some examples from my own *Elite Energy* system as we go along, but remember, what works for me might not work for you. The goal here is not to prescribe a one-size-fits-all solution but to provide you with a framework. I am here to help you define and invest in what will work best for you—what will help you combat burnout and unlock your best capacity and overall well-being.

The person who knows you best is you. Trust that you have the awareness to define what truly supports your well-being and energy.

Now, let's define your *Elite Energy* system!

PART II

DEFINING YOUR SYSTEM

PART II

DEFINING YOUR SYSTEM

CHAPTER 4

FOUNDATIONAL VALUES AND BELIEFS

———

"You cannot get through a single day without having an impact on the world around you. What you do makes a difference, and you have to decide what kind of difference you want to make."

—Jane Goodall

My husband, Neil, has dedicated over twenty years to military service, including seven deployments across Iraq, Kuwait, Qatar, and Afghanistan. Throughout his career, he has been repeatedly called to perform at his highest capacity, even in the face of intense adversity.

Neil's most challenging deployment came just before we met. In the fall of 2014, he was sent to Bagram Air Base in Afghanistan as a logistics specialist, where he endured constant indirect fire from mortars and rockets. A month later, he was forward-deployed to Shindand Air Base, where his team was tasked with overseeing the airlift and removal of all remaining assets, effectively shutting down the base. Initially, the mission was supposed to last just a week or two, with Neil augmenting an already established team. However, after those first two weeks, the team he had joined departed, and Neil and his small crew were left to carry on with the mission, understaffed and without central leadership.

As time went on, more key personnel left, including NATO security forces, which left the base perimeter unsecured. Rations became scarce, the communication infrastructure deteriorated, and even the bathrooms in the passenger terminal, which also served as his living quarters, were overflowing. A month later, after lifting the last remaining equipment onto a military cargo plane, Neil left the forklift on the tarmac, sprinted for the plane, and boarded just as the engines were starting. As the plane corkscrewed upward to avoid possible threats, Neil was not sure if they would make it out alive. When he finally returned to Bagram, Afghanistan, he weighed just 135 pounds at six-foot five-inches—physically and mentally spent, yet somehow still standing.

For Neil, it was his deep-rooted belief in his values, his unwavering focus on the mission, and his clear understanding of *why* he was there that carried him through. Knowing your personal beliefs, values, and principles is so critical that it is one of the central pillars in the United States Air Force's framework, the four pillars of resilience.[1] These pillars are intended to help airmen, like Neil, stay fit, resilient, and mission-ready. The framework emphasizes that connecting to personal *Values & Beliefs* is crucial for developing the perseverance, perspective, and purpose needed to overcome challenges.

Few of us hopefully will ever face the level of pressure Neil experienced during that deployment. However, to break free from burnout and operate with your best capacity, you must understand your *Values & Beliefs*. It is essential to building the energy system you need to protect your well-being, stay focused on your mission, and thrive. It is not just about surviving tough moments; it is about having a deep understanding of what drives you, what truly matters to you, and being able to lean into that strength when the going gets tough.

Your journey toward *Elite Energy* begins with this critical step: identifying your solid foundation. Just as Neil had to know who he was and what he stood for to make it through his most challenging mission, you, too, must identify and define your own personal *Values & Beliefs*.

This is the cornerstone of your *Elite Energy* system. Let's get started.

YOUR FOUNDATION

In the *Elite Energy* system, your foundation is built on your personal **Values & Beliefs**.

Values represent what you hold as important, meaningful, and worthwhile. *Beliefs* are the core convictions that guide your understanding of what is true and trustworthy.

Together, they form the principles that shape your behavior and decisions, giving clarity to what truly matters in your life.

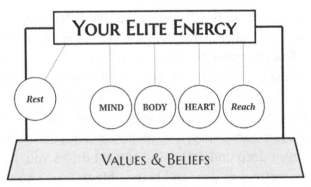

Image 4: Foundational Values & Beliefs (source: Bree Bacon)

When clearly defined, your values and beliefs influence every aspect of your life—how you interact with others, how you lead, and how you navigate challenges. From times of plenty to times of adversity, they serve as a guide, helping you stay grounded and true to yourself.

What you define as your foundation is deeply personal. Choosing the principles that will guide your life and recognizing what you hold as fundamental truths can be a journey, but the choice is yours to make. This self-determined foundation empowers you to live authentically and purposefully, aligning your actions with what you truly believe and value.

As you will see throughout this book, your *Elite Energy* system is a framework. How you fill it out to achieve your personal best capacity is entirely up to you.

WHY IT MATTERS FOR YOUR *ELITE ENERGY*

Understanding and embracing your foundational values and beliefs is essential to unlocking your full potential, optimizing your capacity to do work, and living a life where you thrive. These values are the bedrock of your motivation, decision-making, and well-being. When you are clear about what truly matters to you, it becomes much easier to align your actions with your deeper sense of purpose. This alignment drives not only your capacity and effectiveness but also your satisfaction and sense of fulfillment.

MOTIVATION AND FULFILLMENT

Your values serve as an internal compass, guiding you through the challenges and demands of work. When your daily tasks align with your values, you are more likely to experience passion and motivation, even in the face of difficult assignments. On the other hand, when your work diverges from your core beliefs, it can lead to burnout, frustration, and a sense of disengagement.

In their book *The Burnout Challenge*, Christina Maslach and Michael Leiter identify a mismatch between one's work and personal values as one of the key drivers of burnout. They note that the "moral dimension" of work, how much it resonates with what we deem important, is often underappreciated. Maslach and Leiter emphasize that workers care deeply about "meaningful work that they can feel proud of."[2]

Similarly, research by Adam Grant into "task significance" reveals that understanding the social impact of your work can elevate motivation and performance. In his experiments with fundraising callers and lifeguards, simply highlighting the positive effect of their work on others led to higher job satisfaction and better performance.[3]

Dr. Viktor Frankl, the Austrian psychiatrist and Holocaust survivor, argued the search for meaning is the central motivator in human life. He pointed to studies showing that the overwhelming majority of people value finding meaning in life more than material success.[4] Frankl famously said, "Don't aim at success—the more you aim at it and make it a target, the more you are going to miss it. For success, like happiness, cannot be pursued; it must ensue, and it only does so as the unintended side-effect of one's dedication to a cause greater than oneself."[5]

This perspective underscores the importance of aligning work with a deeper sense of your values and beliefs, which fosters sustained motivation and fulfillment.

DECISION-MAKING CLARITY

Having a clear understanding of your values also provides a solid foundation for making decisions, whether it is prioritizing tasks, navigating ethical dilemmas, or choosing which projects to invest time and energy in. When you know what you stand for, decisions become more straightforward and aligned with your long-term goals. This clarity not only reduces stress but also prevents decision fatigue and internal conflict.

Research actually shows that regularly reflecting on your values helps your stress response. A study looked at participants who "completed either a value-affirmation task or a control task prior to participating in a laboratory stress challenge. Participants who affirmed their values had significantly lower cortisol responses to stress, compared with control participants [...] These findings suggest that reflecting on personal values can keep psychological responses to stress at low levels" when making decisions.[6]

Another study found that college students experiencing high levels of stress were able to solve problems as effectively as students in low-stress conditions when they took a moment to reflect on their most important values.[7] The simple practice of identifying and writing down your values can help you approach tasks with greater focus and clarity, and it can even protect you from the harmful effects of stress.

RESILIENCE AND ADAPTABILITY

As Nelson Mandela famously said, "Do not judge me by my success, judge me by how many times I fell down and got back up again."[8]

True resilience is not just about surviving tough times; it is about staying grounded, drawing strength from a strong sense of self, and using your foundation to navigate adversity and emerge stronger.

Research consistently supports the idea that resilience is rooted in a clear understanding of your values and beliefs. When faced with challenges, having a well-defined set of values provides a sense of direction, allowing you to confront challenges with greater strength and clarity.

For example, research suggests that a strong connection to your *Values & Beliefs* serves as a psychological resource, helping people manage stress and reduce depression and anxiety.[9] Moreover, a solid understanding of your values may enhance your ability to reframe challenges while maintaining hope and meaning.[10]

One compelling study examined the well-being and resilience of cancer patients undergoing chemotherapy during the COVID-19 pandemic. The results revealed that patients who were connected to their values showed greater resilience. They were better able to cope with the compounded stress of their illness and the global crisis, demonstrating that a strong foundation can provide emotional and psychological strength during periods of uncertainty.[11]

Similarly, a study of over five hundred youth in foster care across eleven countries found that a strong connection to one's values was directly linked to higher life satisfaction, better mental health, and increased resilience. Even after accounting for variables such as age, gender, and early adversity, those with a clear sense of their values demonstrated a greater ability to adapt to difficult circumstances and maintain emotional stability.[12]

The underlying message from all of these studies is clear: When we have a deep understanding of our values and beliefs, we are better equipped to navigate stress, uncertainty, and adversity. Our values provide an anchor that helps us make sense of challenges, inform our decisions, fulfill and motivate us, and help us navigate life with resilience and intention.

REFLECT, PROCESS, APPLY

Your turn: We have established that to achieve and sustain your *Elite Energy*, your best capacity, it is essential to define and invest in your foundational *Values & Beliefs*. Now it is time to act. I have designed the following questions and exercises to help you reflect, process, and apply your learnings in a way that allows you to identify and prioritize your personal foundation.

Take a moment to reflect on your current state. On a scale from one to ten, how would you rate yourself in terms of clarity, connection, and consistency in living according to what you value and believe?

Self-Rating

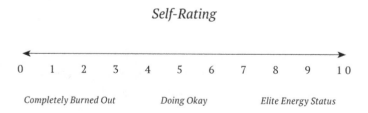

0   1   2   3   4   5   6   7   8   9   1 0

Completely Burned Out   *Doing Okay*   *Elite Energy Status*

Next, answer the following self-assessment questions to help identify areas where you may need more focus or intentionality.

Self-Assessment

1. I have a clear understanding of my foundational *Values & Beliefs.*

   ❏ Yes   ❏ No

2. I feel a connection to something greater than myself.

   ❏ Yes   ❏ No

3. I engage in practices that nurture this connection.

   ❏ Yes   ❏ No

4. My actions consistently align with my personal *Values & Beliefs.*

   ❏ Yes   ❏ No

5. I regularly take time to reflect on my values, beliefs, and actions.

   ❏ Yes   ❏ No

6. I belong to a supportive community or group that fosters a sense of connection to my beliefs.

   ❏ Yes   ❏ No

7. I express my *Values & Beliefs* openly and authentically in both my personal and professional life.

❏ Yes ❏ No

8. My *Values & Beliefs* help me stay grounded and focused, even in times of adversity.

❏ Yes ❏ No

9. When faced with uncertainty, my *Values & Beliefs* give me the strength to stay hopeful and motivated.

❏ Yes ❏ No

10. I derive a sense of meaning and satisfaction from actions that promote my *Values & Beliefs* in the world.

❏ Yes ❏ No

Exercise: Defining Your Foundational Values & Beliefs

Finally, it is time to define your foundational *Values & Beliefs*. If you do not already have a strong sense of your foundation, the following questions will guide you through a reflective process to help bring to mind what truly matters to you. Now is the perfect moment to articulate the principles you want to be the foundation of your *Elite Energy* system.

To start, consider these reflection questions. Take your time, and let your answers come from a place of introspection.

1. **What experiences from your life, upbringing, or culture have most shaped who you are today?**
Think about your family, traditions, cultural influences, and the lessons you have learned along the way. What aspects of your background have had the greatest impact on your identity?

_____

_____

_____

2. **What significant events in your life have profoundly impacted your sense of who you are?**
Reflect on key moments, big or small, that have shaped your worldview or made you reevaluate your identity. These could include challenges you have faced, successes, or turning points that changed the trajectory of your life.

_____

_____

_____

3. **What faith, philosophy, or guiding ideas resonate most deeply with you?**
Consider the belief systems or philosophies that

have shaped your decisions and actions. Whether through religion, spirituality, or personal ideology, what beliefs do you leverage to guide you?

_____

_____

_____

4. How do you want to show up and be remembered?

Think not just about your legacy but how you want people to remember you each day. What do you want your impact to be? How would you like others to perceive you? What actions and values will help you make that vision a reality?

_____

_____

_____

STEP #2: BRAINSTORM

Below is a starting list of some common personal *Values & Beliefs*.[13] Take your time to reflect on each one. Some values may immediately resonate with you, while others may spark new insights or a deeper understanding of what truly matters to you. As you go through the list, highlight or circle the values that speak to you most strongly, and reflect on why they resonate with you personally. Notice any of your personal values or beliefs not listed and write them in.

Accountability	Discipline	Honesty
Achievement	Diversity	Honor
Adventurousness	Dynamism	Humility
Altruism	Effectiveness	Independence
Ambition	Empathy	Inner Harmony
Assertiveness	Enjoyment	Inquisitiveness
Balance	Enthusiasm	Insightfulness
Belonging	Equality	Intelligence
Boldness	Excellence	Intuition
Calmness	Excitement	Joy
Carefulness	Expertise	Justice
Challenge	Exploration	Leadership
Cheerfulness	Expressiveness	Legacy
Clear-Mindedness	Fairness	Loyalty
Commitment	Faith	Mastery
Community	Family	Obedience
Compassion	Fidelity	Openness
Consistency	Fitness	Order
Contentment	Focus	Originality
Contribution	Freedom	Patriotism
Cooperation	Fun	Piety
Courage	Generosity	Positivity
Courtesy	Goodness	Practicality
Creativity	Grace	Preparedness
Curiosity	Growth	Professionalism
Decisiveness	Happiness	Prudence
Dependability	Hard Work	Reliability
Determination	Health	Resourcefulness
Diligence	Holiness	Restraint

Results	Self-Reliance	Unity
Rigor	Sensitivity	Vision
Security	Service	Vitality
Self-Control	Trustworthiness	Fill in the Blank!
Selflessness	Truth-Seeking	

Take some time to reflect and write down the values and beliefs that most resonate with you and why, including any not in the list above.

_____

_____

_____

_____

_____

_____

STEP #3: PRIORITIZATION

Now that you have identified the *Values & Beliefs* that most resonate, it is time to prioritize them. This step is essential for understanding which values truly form the bedrock of your identity and guide your decisions and actions.

Review your list and begin ranking them based on their importance in your life. Consider which ones feel non-negotiable, the *Values & Beliefs* that are absolutely central to who you are and how you want to live.

Once you have ranked them, choose your top one to five that are most fundamental to your identity and character. Go ahead and write them into the foundation of your *Elite Energy* framework.

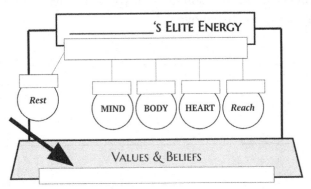

Image 5: Elite Energy Worksheet: Foundational Values & Beliefs (source: Bree Bacon)

For each of the values you select as your top one to five, take time to write down *why* they are so significant to you.

1. _____

2. _____

3. _____

4. _____

5. _____

AN EXAMPLE: BREE'S *ELITE ENERGY*

When I first sat down to complete this exercise for myself, the very first thing that came to mind was my faith, which has been central to my identity since I was young. Along with faith, I reflected on a variety of values that have guided me and given me meaning throughout my life: family, forgiveness, grace, grit, gratitude, thankfulness, service to others, extending love, courage, growth, compassion, and respect.

However, when I had to prioritize and select just five *Values & Beliefs* to represent my foundation, I chose the following:

- **Faith**: Belief in God and living out His message of love and joy.
- **Grit**: Courage, perseverance, and strength in character.
- **Gratitude**: An authentic mindset of appreciation and thankfulness.
- **Growth**: A commitment to continuous learning and self-improvement.
- **Grace**: The ability to extend forgiveness, compassion, and understanding to myself and others.

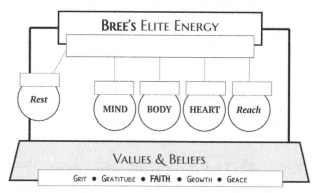

*Image 6: Bree's Elite Energy: Foundational
Values & Beliefs (source: Bree Bacon)*

For me, *faith* is the cornerstone of my life. It is the belief in God and His message of love, joy, and redemption found in the Bible. The two greatest commandments outlined in Matthew 22:37–39 (NIV) guide my purpose and direction: loving God and loving others. Faith anchors my identity and decisions. It shapes how I interact with others, how I approach challenges, and how I see my place in the world. It provides clarity when I am faced with uncertainty, and it is the lens through which I view all things.

Next, I chose *grit* because it represents strength of character, perseverance, and courage in the face of challenges. Grit is the ability to keep pushing forward even when the path is difficult or unclear. My full name, Briana, actually means "strong, virtuous, and honorable," and I want to live up to that. I want my life to reflect courage, not just in moments of triumph but in every effort I make to overcome obstacles, stay committed, and persist even when things are tough.

Gratitude fuels my ability to embrace each moment with appreciation. Practicing gratitude means having an authentic, daily appreciation for the blessings, big and small, in my life. It is about seeing the good even in difficult circumstances, choosing thankfulness over entitlement or negativity. It is about focusing on what is working rather than dwelling on what is lacking. I want to be someone whose gratitude is evident to everyone I meet.

Growth is about the commitment to continuous improvement, learning, and transformation. It is about becoming a better version of myself in every area of life:

spiritually, emotionally, and intellectually. Whether it is pursuing new challenges, expanding my understanding, or learning from failures, growth pushes me to step outside of my comfort zone. It reminds me that no matter where I am today, I can always progress. As long as I have breath, I want to be growing, evolving, and never settling for complacency.

Finally, I chose *grace* as one of my core values because it reminds me of all of our humanity. No one is perfect, and we all make mistakes. I value grace because it reminds me to extend compassion, understanding, and forgiveness to both myself and others. I want to live with the awareness that everyone, including me, is imperfect and flawed, and that true strength comes from the ability to forgive ourselves and others and offer grace in the face of failure or hurt.

These five values form the foundation of my *Elite Energy* framework. They act as a compass, directing my decisions, actions, and interactions with the world. They represent the person I aspire to be each day. By aligning with these values, I gain clarity, motivation, and resilience, allowing me to stay grounded and authentic, whether in moments of success or during life's challenges.

REGULAR REFLECTION: THE KEY TO SUSTAINING YOUR *ELITE ENERGY*

Now that you have identified your foundational *Values & Beliefs*, make regular reflection a part of your routine. Understanding what truly matters to you is only the first step; the next is ensuring that these values remain present and active in your daily life. Regular reflection keeps your foundation strong and ensures that how you show up each and every day consistently aligns with your beliefs.

As you move forward, consider the three simple questions:

1. **Reflect: How can I stay connected to my foundational *Values & Beliefs* today?**
   Remind yourself of the *Values & Beliefs* you have selected and why they matter. Reflect on how these values may show-up in the day to come.

2. **Assess: Where can I improve alignment with my *Values & Beliefs*?**
   Look for areas in your personal or professional life where your actions may be out of sync with your values. Are there behaviors or decisions you could adjust to bring more harmony between what you believe and how you live?

3. **Act: What specific actions can I take to better embody my *Values & Beliefs*?**
   Think of practical steps to reflect your *Values & Beliefs* more intentionally. For example, if growth is a key value, you could seek new challenges that push you outside your comfort zone or find opportunities to collaborate with others who inspire personal development. If service is important, consider dedicating time to volunteering or mentoring others.

As you continue to grow and evolve, so may your *Values & Beliefs*. It is natural for beliefs to shift as you gain new experiences or insights. That is why it is important to revisit your foundation regularly to make sure it still reflects who you are and what you stand for.

For me, personally, I start each day with a commitment to reflect. I carve out quiet time every morning (often with a cup of coffee in hand) to ground myself, reminding myself of who I am, what I stand for, and how I want to show up in the world. While I may not always live perfectly according to my values, this daily moment of self-reflection acts as an anchor, helping me align my actions throughout the day with my foundational beliefs.

My husband, Neil, has a similar ritual. He set a daily calendar reminder for himself that reads: "Take your time. Be kind. Be thoughtful. Be authentic. You have a job to do. Do it well and be thankful, but relax. God loves you as you are. Ask questions and take notes. Keep Eliana's (our daughter's) laughter in your head."

This reminder helps him stay focused on what matters most: being present, staying grounded, and living with intention. These practices, small as they may seem, ensure your day-to-day actions reflect what you value and are the anchor of your *Elite Energy* system.

By consistently reflecting on your *Values & Beliefs*, you reinforce their influence over your decisions and actions. These foundational principles serve as your compass, ensuring you live in alignment with what you believe and strive to represent.

CONGRATULATIONS!

You have successfully completed the foundation of your *Elite Energy* system. By identifying your *Values & Beliefs*, reflecting on them regularly, and making them a part of your daily life, you are laying a strong foundation for living with purpose and authenticity.

Now that you have reflected on your *Values & Beliefs*, consider inspiring others. Share your foundation with the hashtag #YourEliteEnergy_Foundation.

Next up, we will move on to define the *core* of your *Elite Energy* system: your **Mind, Body,** and **Heart**. Keep going. Your journey to your best capacity and overall well-being is just beginning.

CHAPTER 5

CORE I—MIND

"There is no health without mental health."

—Dr. David Satcher

Lieutenant Colonel Kurt Steinmetz is no stranger to pressure. As the commander of the 133rd Logistics Readiness Squadron in the Minnesota Air National Guard, he has spent over two decades leading in the high-stakes world of military operations. His job is about more than logistics and readiness; it is about the well-being of the airmen under his command.

In a conversation with me he discussed how many airmen enlist at just seventeen years old, still in their senior year of high school. For some, drill weekends—the one weekend each month that traditional National Guard members serve—are the most stable and supportive environment they experience all month. This awareness weighs heavily on him, as he is responsible for their military readiness ensuring they are prepared to serve their country, which includes looking after their well-being. It is a significant mental load to bear.

One example he shared with me was when he served as a notification officer, a role that closely resembles what you see in movies. When a service member died, he was tasked with driving to the loved one's home in uniform, knocking on the door, and delivering the heartbreaking news. He recalls a particular young airman whose death continues to haunt him, a twenty-one-year old deployed in Germany who took his own life. "I couldn't even make eye contact with the parents. I just read the letter exactly as it was written. That one still bothers me today," he shared.

To prioritize his personal mental health, Lt. Col. Steinmetz has made it a point throughout his career to establish a clear boundary between work and home life. When he is at work, he is fully focused, but he also strives to leave work behind when he heads home. Having experienced a previous boss known for sending emails at all hours, even at 11:00 p.m. or 3:00 a.m., Lt. Col. Steinmetz understands the pressure of feeling "always on." To counter this, he makes a point of visibly leaving the office, signaling to his team they should also prioritize their home lives.

Yet, despite these efforts, like many of us, his mind can race at night with thoughts of how to problem solve or reflections on the day's challenges. He can find himself searching for ways to tackle various issues, leading to a cycle of worry and anxiety that can make it difficult to relax and recharge.

To ensure he is at his personal best leadership capacity, he has developed creative wellness strategies to shift his mind away from work in the evenings.

Curious about his approach?

I will share his personal mental wellness practices before the chapter concludes.

First, the *core* of your *Elite Energy* system includes your *Mind*, *Body*, and *Heart*. We are going to start with what you do to protect and invest in your incredible **Mind**.

CORE I: YOUR MIND

The **Mind** in your *Elite Energy* system represents your mental health and wellness. It encompasses your ability to think, feel, perceive, imagine, remember, and exercise willpower—the full spectrum of your mental faculties.

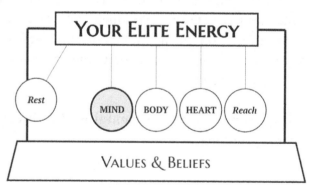

Image 7: Core I: Your Mind (source: Bree Bacon)

Mental *health* is more than just the absence of mental illness. According to the World Health Organization, "Mental health is a state of mental well-being that enables people to cope with the stresses of life, realize their abilities, learn well and work well, and contribute to their community."[1]

Mental *wellness* involves the regular habits and practices that support and nurture your mental health. This is where we will focus our attention, exploring the importance of regular wellness routines and practices that enhance your mental health and contribute to the vitality of your overall *Elite Energy* system.

WHY IT MATTERS FOR YOUR *ELITE ENERGY*

A 2024 study by The Harris Poll reveals that more than over a third of full-time employed Americans, 35 percent, report that stress related to their mental health negatively impacts their work performance. That is a higher percentage than those stressed about physical health, job security, social issues, or caregiving.[2] Additionally, "76 percent of US workers reported at least one symptom of a mental health condition."[3] This highlights the critical need for a focus on our mental health and wellness, as research consistently shows that doing so is key to unlocking our *Elite Energy*.

Below are some ways your mental health directly influences your capacity.

COGNITIVE FUNCTION

Cognitive function refers to the mental processes that allow us to acquire knowledge, manipulate information, and reason effectively. These include essential skills such as perception, memory, learning, attention, decision-making, and language abilities. All of these cognitive functions are critical to your best capacity, your ability to make an impact.

A 2021 meta-analysis by researchers highlights the significant impact of burnout on cognitive functioning. Key abilities such as memory, focus, verbal skills, and multitasking are notably impaired. Individuals struggle with recalling information, maintaining attention, and switching between tasks. Impulse control declines, leading to increased irritability and impatience. Additionally, burnout reduces executive functioning, learning capacity, and the ability to process new information, underscoring the critical importance of prioritizing mental wellness to preserve cognitive performance.[4]

Llewellyn E. van Zyl, a professor of positive psychology at North-West University, studies the factors that enhance mental health. He explains, "Your brain isn't built for the relentless strain of nonstop overwork. This overexposure to chronic work-related stress results in excess levels of cortisol being pumped into your system, which not only wears out your mental energy but causes your brain to literally short-circuit and shrink."[5]

ADAPTABILITY AND RESILIENCE

Industries and workplaces are constantly evolving. Whether driven by technological advancements, market shifts, or societal changes, the ability to navigate unexpected challenges and adapt is essential. We have discussed how your foundational values and beliefs support resilience, but so does investing in your mental health and wellness.

Research shows a strong link between mental wellness practices and improved resilience and adaptability. For example, a recent study focused on mindfulness training and its impact on resilience in millennials. The results confirmed that mindfulness not only enhanced psychological health but also strengthened resilience, supporting previous findings that mental wellness boosts our ability to adapt.[6]

Suzette Brémault-Phillips, an associate professor in Rehabilitation Medicine at the University of Alberta, highlights the connection between resilience and mental health. She explains, "These things seem so small— going for a walk, getting out in the sunshine, expressing gratitude, lending a helping hand—and yet what it does is it actually changes our biochemistry and our thinking processes. It gives us a break and enables us to look at things in a different way."[7]

EMOTIONAL REGULATION

Mental health is often mistakenly equated with always being happy, but this is simply not the case. It is completely normal to feel sad, unwell, angry, or upset at times. These emotions are part of living a full and authentic life. What a solid mental wellness routine helps with is regulating these emotions and responding to them in a healthy, productive way.

Take gratitude as an example. Gratitude involves consciously focusing on and appreciating the positive aspects of life, whether large or small. A 2015 study using MRI scans found that practicing gratitude led to increased activity in the prefrontal cortex, the brain region involved in decision-making, emotions, and social behavior. This suggests that gratitude has a direct effect on our emotional regulation processes.[8]

In a study published in the *Journal of Positive Psychology*, researchers had undergraduate students engage in a journaling exercise twice a week for four weeks. Participants either wrote about gratitude or focused on every day, non-emotional experiences. Afterward, they were shown a series of positive and negative images. The results showed that those who had written about gratitude were better at managing their emotional reactions to the negative images. The researchers suggested that gratitude helped participants cultivate a general positive attitude toward life, which in turn protected their emotional state.[9] This demonstrates how a simple practice like regularly expressing gratitude can enhance emotional regulation and improve your decision-making skills.

MENTAL WELLNESS CONSIDERATIONS

Investing in your mental health and wellness is undeniably important. So, *how* do you invest in your mental wellness? To help guide you, below we explore different practices to consider. This is not an exhaustive list but rather a starting point.

Remember, this is your system. What works for me or someone else may not be the best fit for you. *Your Elite Energy* is the framework, and how you personalize it is entirely up to you.

What follows is a brief introduction to various wellness practices. Each discipline could likely fill an entire book on its own. Think of this section as a collection of thought starters to help you explore and define the mental wellness habits and practices that will best support your *Elite Energy*.

JOURNALING

Journaling is a powerful mental wellness practice with numerous benefits. Studies show that regular "journaling about our deepest thoughts and feelings can even reduce the number of sick days we take off work."[10] Research also suggests "journaling can help us accept rather than judge our mental experiences, resulting in fewer negative emotions in response to stressors."[11]

A variety of techniques can be leveraged. Below are some common exercises to consider.

> **Stream of consciousness**: Stream of consciousness journaling is all about writing without constraints. It is about letting go of expectations, goals, and judgment—just write. The key is to let whatever is in your mind flow onto the page. This exercise can help you clear your mind and process your emotions. If you need a prompt, here are a few to get you started:

- What was the best thing that happened today?
- What was the worst thing that happened?
- What was the most interesting thing I saw or heard?
- What was the most challenging thing I faced?
- What were the feelings and emotions I experienced?
- What triggered those feelings and emotions?

Unsent letter: If you are feeling particularly hurt or angry, try writing a letter to express your feelings, one you never send. This exercise allows you to articulate your emotions honestly without the pressure of resolution or confrontation. A friend of mine swears by this practice. When she feels upset by someone or something, she writes a letter explaining her feelings but never mails it. Writing it down helps her process and move past the situation, allowing her to let go of anger or hurt and gain mental clarity.

Gratitude: Gratitude journaling is a practice focused on recognizing and appreciating the positive aspects of your life. It is a simple yet powerful way to shift your focus from negative thoughts to the good things you might otherwise overlook. You do not need to be a skilled writer, just jot down the things you are grateful for, whether big or small. Since gratitude is one of my foundational values, this practice is a favorite of mine. When I feel down or frustrated, taking a moment to reflect on what I am grateful for helps me reframe my mindset and improve my mental state. It is a quick but effective way to ground myself in thankfulness and reset my emotional balance.

One word: If you do not consider yourself a writer, like me, try a simple practice called one-word journaling. This involves reflecting on an experience or your day and capturing it with just one word that summarizes your feelings. It can be a quick and powerful exercise that helps you process emotions without the pressure of writing long entries. You can make it a daily habit, choosing one word that encapsulates how you felt about the day. It is an easy, no-frills way to track your mental wellness and gain insights into your emotional state.

Cognitive behavioral therapy (CBT) thought record: CBT is a common type of therapy designed to help you identify and challenge negative thought patterns. A CBT thought record is an excellent journaling exercise to support this goal. Here is how it works:[12]

- **Situation**: What happened?
- **Your feelings**: How did you feel in the moment?
- **Unhelpful thoughts**: What negative or unhelpful thoughts came to mind?
- **Evidence supporting**: What evidence can you find that supports those negative thoughts?
- **Evidence against**: What evidence contradicts those thoughts?
- **Alternatives**: What are more neutral or realistic thoughts you could adopt?
- **How you feel now**: How do you feel after completing the exercise?

MINDFULNESS

Mindfulness refers to the practice of being fully present in the moment, calmly acknowledging and accepting your thoughts, emotions, and bodily sensations. It often involves techniques like breathing exercises, guided imagery, and other practices to help center your mind and alleviate stress. Research has shown that mindfulness can reduce stress, anxiety, pain, depression, insomnia, and high blood pressure. It can also improve focus, decrease job burnout, and enhance sleep quality.[13]

Earlier in chapter 3, I shared one of my favorite mindfulness exercises, the 5-4-3-2-1 technique. Below is one more simple mindfulness breathing exercise that has supported me in managing anxiety, panic, and PTSD. You may find your own preferred mindfulness techniques that work best for you.

> **Box breathing**: Box breathing is a simple and powerful technique for calming your mind, especially in stressful situations. It involves four steps—inhale, hold, exhale, hold—each for a count of four. This exercise helps to regulate your breath, reduce stress, and bring focus to the present moment.
>
> Consider trying it right now.
>
> - Inhale for a count of four.
> - Hold your breath for a count of four.

- Exhale slowly for a count of four.
- Hold your exhale for a count of four.

Repeat for several rounds. I first used box breathing when I began experiencing panic attacks, and it has since become one of my go-to techniques for calming my body and mind in moments of stress.

SILENCE

In our increasingly noisy world, filled with traffic, construction, background music, podcasts, and constant social media scrolling, it is easy to forget the power of silence. Yet, research and experts alike confirm that time spent in silence can offer numerous health benefits. Silence has been shown to lower blood pressure, improve concentration and focus, calm racing thoughts, stimulate brain growth, reduce cortisol, and even enhance creativity.[14]

For me, incorporating more silence into my daily routine has been incredibly helpful. When anxiety or panic starts to rise, I find that stepping into a quiet space, whether it is a calm room or a peaceful outdoor setting, helps me disconnect from overstimulation. Being in nature, with its sights, smells, and sounds, offers a mental reset. I can just breathe and create space for stillness in my mind.

When was the last time you experienced true silence?

If it has been a while, try to create small moments of stillness in your day. For instance, you could make your vehicle a noise-free zone, where you commit to not listening to music or podcasts during your commute. Perhaps wake up a few minutes earlier before the rest of your household rises to enjoy a quiet morning. Even a simple five-minute break with just a cup of coffee, tea, or water—no phone, email, or distractions—can be an instant refresh for your mind and spirit.

BREAKS

For my friends in Corporate America, this one is for you. How many of us have back-to-back meetings... all... day... long?

Meetings run over, we skip meals, and sometimes we barely have a moment to even use the bathroom. We do not take time to breathe, let alone take a proper break. However, taking breaks is essential for maintaining your best capacity.

According to research from the University of North Carolina, when we work hard, our brain must resist distractions to stay focused. The prefrontal cortex, which controls concentration, logical thinking, and impulse control, takes on a lot of work during intense focus. As we push through task after task, our brain expends energy, and our ability to concentrate weakens.[15] At some point, we need to recharge. Rather than powering through, taking regular breaks actually increases productivity and helps maintain your capacity over the long haul.

The first step is to actively schedule breaks into your day. One practice that works for me is blocking twenty- to thirty-minute intervals on my calendar in the morning and afternoon, so my day is not completely booked with meetings. I also block time for lunch every day. If that is hard to do, consider scheduling meetings to start five minutes after the hour or end ten minutes earlier. These small adjustments can ensure you get the mental space you need.

Second, make sure your breaks are quality ones. Simply scrolling through social media is not the most effective way to recharge. You want to return from your break feeling refreshed and ready to focus. Quality breaks could involve something physical (like stretching or walking), something relaxing (listening to music or doing a quick mindfulness exercise), or something social (a chat with a colleague, friend, or family member). The key is to engage in an activity that helps you step away from your work, recharge, and return to your tasks with renewed focus and energy.

Taking breaks is not a luxury; it is a productivity strategy. Make sure to give yourself permission to pause, reset, and come back to your work stronger.

INVEST IN JOY

When was the last time you did something purely for the joy of it? It is easy to forget in our "always on" culture, but play and leisure are vital for relieving stress, improving brain function, and sparking creativity.[16] Maybe it is re-reading a favorite book, watching a classic movie, or playing with your kids or pets. You could check out a new museum exhibit, attend a sporting event, or host a game night. Even learning a new skill, not for work but just for fun, can be a great way to inject some joy into your life.

A development editor I worked with on this book shared his own story of investing in joy. A few years ago, he discovered that all the software needed to create professional video games was available for free. He began coding, 3D modeling, and animating games—combining "fun" with just enough challenge to keep him engaged. What he did not expect was how these new skills would enhance his day job. He ended up learning multiple coding languages and even some trigonometry, something he never imagined would benefit his career. By working in a new medium, he gained a fresh perspective on storytelling, which ultimately improved his work in writing and editing.

Research also supports the value of joy. A study at Oxford found that happy employees are 13 percent more productive.[17] Similarly, in a recent study by BYU, information systems professors found that work teams who spent just forty-five minutes playing games together saw a 20 percent increase in productivity on subsequent tasks.[18]

If you want *Elite Energy*, your best capacity, do not underestimate the power of play. Take time to enjoy life. Have some fun.

BOUNDARIES

Do you have healthy boundaries? I will be honest: I am still working on this myself. If you are a people-pleaser or an achiever (or both), it can be especially tough. We often feel compelled to say yes to everything, whether it is at work, with family, or with friends. However, healthy boundaries are crucial for maintaining self-esteem, avoiding burnout, and preserving your sense of identity.[19] This is not just important at work but also with family and friends. Setting boundaries allows you to take control of your time and energy, ensuring you are showing up as your best self in all areas of life.

The first boundary to consider is saying no. It sounds simple, but it can be incredibly difficult. Saying no does not have to be harsh or disrespectful. It is about prioritizing your time and energy. For work, priorities can change constantly, with more work than hours in the day. A great way to set boundaries is to ask where the new task or project falls on the priority list. You might say something like, "I would be happy to take this one on, but that means I won't be able to submit the report by Friday. Can it wait another week?" This allows you to stay in control of your workload without overcommitting.

Another boundary is managing late-night or early-morning meetings. For those of us with colleagues in multiple time zones, this can be particularly challenging. I know from personal experience that these meetings can eat into precious time with loved ones. For me, I had to make the difficult decision to decline late-night and early-morning calls because they were cutting into the limited hours I had with my daughter. It was not easy, but

I learned to lean on others to represent in those meetings or to prioritize only the most critical ones.

A final boundary I would recommend is being selective about the meetings you attend. Often we are tempted to be present in every meeting to ensure we are not missing out on crucial information or context. However, if you are going to maintain the space and energy to do your best work, you need to be selective about where you show up. Consider whether you truly need to be in every meeting. One approach I take is to delegate meeting attendance. You could say, "I'm going to have [name] represent our team's perspective at this meeting and be responsible for sharing key insights and action items afterward."

One colleague shared with me the concept of creating a culture of JOMO (joy of missing out), which flips the idea of FOMO (fear of missing out) on its head. In this culture, missing out on unnecessary meetings or tasks is actually a source of joy, because it frees up your time and energy for what really matters.

RETURN TO OUR STORY

Let's return to Lt. Col. Steinmetz. During our conversation, I was struck by the immense responsibility he carries as a leader, tasked with ensuring the readiness of all the airmen under his charge. I asked him how he personally copes with it all.

He shared that one of his strategies for managing the mental load is to engage in activities that require his focus but are unrelated to his work. For instance, he took up crochet in the evenings. "It's interesting, my brain can't focus on work when my hands are busy with something else," he explained. He and his wife also share a love for reading, diving into books together at night and discussing the ideas they come across, which provides a refreshing break from his daily responsibilities. He has even signed up for a beekeeping class as a new hobby, learning an entirely different skillset that helps him decompress.

However, his primary wellness practice for mental health is ensuring he carves out time for himself. Whether it is a weekend spent hunting, working alone in his garage, or simply enjoying a quiet moment of solitude, he knows that given the weight of leading so many service members, he must prioritize these moments of rest and restoration. By doing so, he ensures he can maintain his energy and serve at his highest capacity. This sense of balance remains key for his ability to perform at his best, both personally and professionally.

REFLECT, PROCESS, APPLY
Your turn: Do you have any mental wellness practices that work particularly well for you? Perhaps it's a different type of journaling, a specific mindfulness exercise, or a unique practice that helps you maintain mental clarity and emotional balance. Whatever it is, the next step is to define your personal *Mind* commitment, at least one consistent practice that supports your *Elite Energy* system.

First, take a moment to reflect: How are you doing right now? If you were to rate your current mental health, your state of being, on a scale of one to ten, where would you place yourself today?

Self-Rating

| 0 | 1 | 2 | 3 | 4 | 5 | 6 | 7 | 8 | 9 | 1 0 |

Completely Burned Out   *Doing Okay*   *Elite Energy Status*

Next, how are you doing today in maintaining regular wellness habits and practices that support your mental health and overall *Elite Energy* system?

Self-Assessment

1. I set boundaries to protect my personal time and prevent overwork.

   ❏ Yes ❏ No

2. I take breaks throughout the day to recharge.

   ❏ Yes ❏ No

3. I regularly engage in activities that bring me joy and fulfillment.

   ❏ Yes ❏ No

4. I regularly make time for self-reflection (such as journaling or meditation).

   ❏ Yes ❏ No

5. I make space to listen to my thoughts, judgments, beliefs, attitudes, and feelings.

❏ Yes ❏ No

6. I say "no" to extra responsibilities sometimes.

❏ Yes ❏ No

7. I engage my intelligence in a new area (like visiting a museum, history exhibit, sports event, theater performance; taking a new class; or learning a new skill).

❏ Yes ❏ No

8. I allow myself space to be curious.

❏ Yes ❏ No

9. I actively challenge negative thoughts and practice positive self-talk.

❏ Yes ❏ No

10. I allow myself to experience a range of emotions and express them.

❏ Yes ❏ No

Exercise: Start, Stop, Continue

The "Start, Stop, Continue" exercise is a simple but powerful reflection tool I often used in my corporate experience to evaluate and adjust behaviors. In this case, we will apply it to the habits and practices that support your *Mind* and mental wellness.

Reflect on the following questions and consider any adjustments you need to make to ensure your mental health is optimized for your best capacity and overall well-being.

1. **Are there any habits or practices regarding my mental wellness that I want to *continue*?**
   Reflect on the positive habits and practices that already support your mental health; that help you feel at your best. What are the things you do regularly that contribute to a calm, focused, and healthy state of mind?

   Example: "I want to continue journaling every morning to clear my mind before I start my day."

   _____

   _____

   _____

2. **Are there any habits or practices that I should *stop* to better support my mental health?**
   Identify any habits, activities, or mindsets that might be draining your mental energy or

contributing to stress, anxiety, or burnout. What is not serving you anymore?

Example: "I should stop checking my email first thing in the morning, as it creates unnecessary stress and disrupts my focus."

_____

_____

_____

3. **Are there any habits or practices that I should consider *starting* to better support my mental health?**
What new habits, behaviors, or practices could help you take better care of your *Mind*? What changes or additions could give you more mental clarity, emotional balance, and overall well-being?

Example: "I should start incorporating daily mindfulness exercises, like deep breathing or meditation, to reduce anxiety and improve my focus."

_____

_____

_____

4. **Given my assessment, my** *number one* **commitment for my** *Mind* **is...**
Based on your reflection, identify your most important commitment to your mental wellness moving forward. What one habit or practice will you prioritize that will have the biggest impact on your mental health and overall well-being?

Example: "My number one commitment is to prioritize regular breaks during my workday to recharge and avoid burnout."

---

5. **This is my number one commitment because...**
Reflect on why this habit is so important to you. Consider how it will improve your mental health, boost your energy, and enhance your performance or well-being.

Example: "Taking breaks regularly is crucial because it allows me to stay focused and maintain high energy levels throughout the day, preventing burnout and promoting my best capacity."

AN EXAMPLE: BREE'S *ELITE ENERGY*

For my mental health and wellness assessment, a habit I want to *continue* is the box breathing and the 5-4-3-2-1 technique. Both of these practices help me stay grounded and manage stress. A habit I want to *stop* is checking my work email first thing in the morning. It tends to overwhelm me right out of the gate and sets a stressful tone for the day. Lastly, a habit I want to *start* is making more space for pure fun, whether that is exploring new hobbies, spending quality time with loved ones, or simply being present in the moment.

However, my number one *Mind* commitment for my *Elite Energy* system is taking regular breaks. Stepping away from my work, whether for a short walk, stretching, or just a moment of quiet reflection, allows me to reset, recharge, and ultimately come back to my tasks with more clarity and focus. I have found that breaks are essential for maintaining my mental clarity and productivity throughout the day. To have my best capacity, I need to prioritize these moments to recharge and come back with an improved ability to focus.

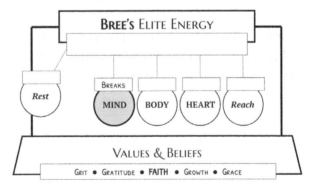

Image 8: Bree's Mind Commitment—Breaks (source: Bree Bacon)

AMAZING WORK! YOUR MIND COMMITMENT IS SET

Go ahead and write your number one commitment for your *Mind* into your *Elite Energy* framework, available to print at www.BreeBacon.com.[20]

You have just made an important step toward prioritizing your mental health and optimizing your *Elite Energy*. Writing down your number one commitment for your *Mind* is a powerful tool for maintaining focus and motivation as you continue to invest in your overall well-being.

Now that you have reflected on what works for you, the next step is to integrate these practices into your regular routine. Why not inspire others to do the same? Share your commitment with the hashtag #YourEliteEnergy_Mind. Encourage your community to join you on this journey toward improved mental health and wellness.

NEXT UP: INVESTING IN YOUR *BODY*

Now that you have defined your commitment for your *Mind*, it is time to turn our focus to the next component in your *Elite Energy* system: how to invest in your **Body**. Take a moment to congratulate yourself for prioritizing your mental health and wellness, completing part I of III for a stronger, more energized version of the *core* of your *Elite Energy* system.

CHAPTER 6

CORE II—BODY

———

*"Take care of your body. It's the
only place you have to live."*

—JIM ROHN

My friend, Mark, is the founder and CEO of Custom Box Agency, an innovative company that creates unique, experiential boxes for clients. He is passionate about his work, his team, and his clients. However, he admits that building and running a business can take its toll.

By 2023, Mark had built a highly successful business, but his personal health was beginning to suffer. As he puts it, "I was stressed out, couldn't sleep at night, and my health was deteriorating." At that time, he was in constant pain, and his body fat percentage had climbed above 35 percent, classifying him as morbidly obese. The idea of seeing a doctor filled him with dread, as he did not want to face the reality that something might be seriously wrong with his health.

Then one morning, everything changed. While chatting with his executive assistant, Mark suddenly experienced an aura in his vision. It began as a flicker of light on the right side of his field of vision and gradually spread, distorting everything around him. Though he could still see, the world seemed blurry and distorted, and panic set in. His heart raced as he tried to search online to figure out what was happening. "According to Google, I was either having a stroke or experiencing an ocular migraine," he recalls. Thankfully, his assistant recognized the signs—Mark was having his first ocular migraine.

That moment was a wake-up call. Mark realized that in order for his business to continue thriving, he needed to invest in himself, particularly his physical health and wellness. He understood that to be the best leader he could be, he needed to prioritize his own well-being, enabling him to lead his team effectively and sustainably.

Before we go deeper into Mark's inspiring journey, let's explore the research that highlights the importance of taking care of your **Body**, your physical health and wellness, as a *core* element of fueling your *Elite Energy* system.

CORE II: YOUR BODY
The **Body** in your *Elite Energy* system represents your *physical* health and wellness. Our bodies are capable of a vast range of functions: We move, heal, digest, breathe, protect, grow, and even reproduce—just to name a few.

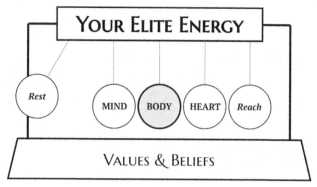

Image 9: Core II: Your Body (source: Bree Bacon)

Your physical *health* stands for your current or desired state of being. Similar to mental health, physical health is not simply the absence of disease or illness. Instead, it is a state in which all the internal and external components of your body (organs, muscles, tissues, and cells) function to the best of your individual ability, supporting you to live and thrive according to your own potential.[1]

Your physical *wellness* refers to the regular habits and practices that support your physical health. We will focus our attention here, on the importance of consistent wellness practices that help you maintain and improve your personal physical health, allowing you to function at your best and fuel your overall energy.

WHY IT MATTERS FOR YOUR *ELITE ENERGY*

Researchers in the United Kingdom analyzed over thirty thousand employees across 173 organizations as part of the annual *Britain's Healthiest Workplace* survey. The results revealed that physical health, along with mental health, was responsible for more than 84 percent of the direct impact on productivity loss, along with 93 percent of indirect influences.[2] This underscore just how critical it is to invest in your physical health and wellness to fuel your best capacity.

Below are ways your physical health directly influences your energy and overall well-being.

MENTAL HEALTH

Investing in your physical wellness has a direct and powerful impact on your mental health. Physical activity stimulates the release of endorphins, neurotransmitters that promote feelings of happiness and well-being, while also reducing stress and anxiety.[3] Quality sleep is essential for cognitive functions such as attention, concentration, and decision-making.[4] Additionally, consuming nutrients like vitamins, minerals, omega-3 fatty acids, and antioxidants supports brain function and neurotransmitter production, which help regulate your mood and emotions.[5]

A study from Australia aimed to quantify the impact of physical health on an individual's mental health. Researchers analyzed data from nearly twenty-five thousand individuals in the *Household Income and Labour Dynamics in Australia* (HILDA) survey. They found that even a one-point improvement in physical health scores led to a corresponding 43 percent increase in participants' mental health scores.[6]

The best part is you do not need to add intensive exercise or extreme diets to experience these benefits. Experts agree that no matter your age or fitness level, any amount of physical improvement can boost your mental health.[7]

RESILIENCE

As we have explored throughout our journey, resilience is essential to achieving and maintaining your best capacity. Life is full of challenges, whether it is dealing with health issues, changes in job, income, or housing, the loss of loved ones, or the isolation that can come from separation from loved ones. Adversity is unfortunately inevitable, but how we respond to it can make all the difference.

One of the most powerful ways to build resilience is by investing in your physical health and wellness. Research shows that physical exercise enhances resilience by releasing endorphins, the body's natural mood boosters, which help reduce stress hormones like cortisol.[8] As discussed above, this not only helps to manage stress but also improves overall mental health. Regular physical activity also promotes neuroplasticity, which is the brain's ability to form new connections and adapt to challenges.[9] This process strengthens cognitive function and supports emotional stability, making it easier to handle life's ups and downs.

Equally important to building resilience is ensuring quality sleep. The American Psychological Association points out that adults who get less than eight hours of sleep per night are more prone to experiencing stress-related symptoms, such as irritability, anger, lack of motivation, and feeling overwhelmed. These individuals may also find themselves losing patience with loved ones or skipping exercise, and they are more likely to report an increase in stress over the past year.[10]

Prioritizing your physical health and wellness is clearly essential for having resilience, maintaining emotional balance, and managing stress effectively.

DISEASE AND ILLNESSES

Finally, investing in your physical wellness plays a crucial role in enhancing your ability to fight and prevent diseases and illnesses. Regular physical activity also provides powerful anti-inflammatory effects, which help protect against chronic diseases linked to ongoing inflammation, such as autoimmune disorders, certain cancers, heart disease, and high blood pressure.[11]

In fact, an increasing number of doctors are now encouraging patients to view physical wellness as a key strategy for fighting or overcoming diseases, rather than relying on medication alone. A study published in the *British Medical Journal* found that exercise can have outcomes for certain serious medical conditions that are comparable to prescription drugs. For example, exercise led to better recovery outcomes in patients rehabilitating after a stroke, and for individuals with coronary heart disease and pre-diabetes, exercise and medication showed similar results.[12]

This is not to suggest that you should stop taking prescribed medications, as these remain essential for the successful treatment of many conditions. However, these studies highlight the growing recognition of physical wellness practices as an effective, complementary strategy for fighting disease and improving overall health. Incorporating exercise into your routine can play a significant role in both prevention and recovery.

PHYSICAL WELLNESS CONSIDERATIONS

Investing in your physical health and wellness is essential, but *how* do you actually go about it? What practical steps can you take to improve your physical health and, in turn, boost your overall best capacity?

To help guide you, we will focus on the core three: exercise, nutrition, and sleep. While these may seem like basic elements, I came across a journal article during my research for this book that reminded even medical students, those who are highly knowledgeable about health, about the fundamental importance of nutrition, sleep, and exercise. Despite their expertise, the stress of medical school often leads students to neglect these basics.[13] Even those of us in professions dedicated to the health and well-being of others can sometimes lose sight of the essentials that fuel our own *Elite Energy*.

Remember that your *Elite Energy* system is uniquely yours. What works for me, or for someone else, may not be the best approach for you. The framework is universal, but how you fill it out is deeply personal. As we discuss nutrition, exercise, and sleep, I encourage you to reflect on what works best for you so you can tailor these practices to your own needs and overall well-being.

NUTRITION

I have chosen to use the word "nutrition" rather than "diet" for a reason. For many, "diet" can feel synonymous with restriction, but I prefer to think of what we put into our bodies as fuel for our capacity. Just like a car needs the right fuel to run smoothly, your body requires the right nutrients to function at its best.

Hippocrates famously said, "Let thy food be thy medicine and thy medicine be thy food."[14] Over two thousand years later, modern science continues to support this wisdom. What you eat impacts nearly every aspect of your *Body*, from your brain and immune system to your physical abilities and overall health.[15] For example, the foods you consume can directly influence the quality and duration of your sleep. Caffeine, for instance, can make it harder to fall asleep, while "eating too close to bedtime can lead to sleep disruptions."[16] Foods high in calories or unhealthy fats can also interfere with restful sleep, as can nutrient deficiencies, such as a lack of calcium, magnesium, and vitamins A, C, D, and E.[17]

According to Harvard's Center for Wellness and Health Promotion, your food choices play a critical role in boosting your energy, productivity, mood, and self-esteem.[18] Alongside a lack of physical activity, the World Health

Organization has identified unhealthy eating habits as one of the leading global risk factors for poor health.[19]

How often have we skipped a meal because back-to-back meetings leave no time to eat, or mindlessly snacked on whatever is within reach to keep us going as we try to power through our never-ending to-do lists?

As Dr. Mark Hyman puts it, "What most people don't realize is that food is not just calories; it's information. It actually contains messages that connect to every cell in the body."[20] What you put into your body sends signals that shape how you feel, think, and perform.

Nutrition is deeply personal, but you will find no shortage of opinions on what is best to eat for optimal well-being. I am not here to endorse any one approach to nutrition. My goal is simply to emphasize that what you eat is a key component of your best capacity, your *Elite Energy*. Regularly evaluating what foods and eating habits nourish your *Body* and support your unique needs is important.

A few things to consider:

- *Balance and variety*: Is your food intake balanced? Your *Body* needs a range of essential nutrients, including vitamins, minerals, healthy fats, carbohydrates, and proteins, to function optimally. A varied diet is important for maintaining health at all levels. For example, research from the American Gut Project found that individuals who ate a greater variety of plant-based foods had healthier gut microbiomes, which is linked to better digestion, brain function, and immune resilience.[21]

- *Hydration*: Water is crucial for so many of your physical functions, from nutrient absorption to regulating temperature and eliminating waste. Staying hydrated is essential for overall health. The United States National Academies of Sciences recommends that adults consume between 11.5 to 15.5 cups of water a day, depending on factors like physical activity and climate.[22]

- *Mindful Eating*: How often do you eat while distracted? Whether at your desk, in a meeting, or rushing through errands, eating without truly paying attention to your hunger and fullness signals can lead to overeating or missing out on the joy of your food. Carl Honoré, a bestselling author and advocate for the slow movement (a cultural initiative advocating for a reduction in the pace of modern life) notes, "In our fast-forward culture, we have lost the art of eating well. Food is often little more than fuel to pour down the hatch while doing other stuff—surfing the web, driving, walking along the street. Dining al desko is now the norm in many workplaces. All of this speed takes a toll."[23] Taking time to slow down and savor your food helps you better tune into your needs.

Ultimately, nutrition is a vital piece of your capacity. It is worth taking the time to explore how different foods and eating patterns make you feel, and adjust your habits accordingly to fuel your *Body* in the best possible way.

SLEEP

Did you know that staying awake for twenty-four hours straight has the same physical effect as having a blood-alcohol concentration of 0.1 percent?[24] That is above the legal driving limit in most of the United States.

This topic is personal for me. When the demands of life and leadership pile up, I have found myself lying awake at night, trying to problem-solve or plan for the day ahead. If I am still wide awake at 2:00, 3:00, and 4:00 a.m., I convince myself that since I am not sleeping, I might as well be productive and get some work done. The truth is, consistently getting at least seven hours of quality sleep is essential for your best capacity to feel sharp, energized, and ready to tackle each day.

Sleep is not a luxury. It is a biological necessity. Yet more than a third of Americans get less than seven hours of sleep a night.[25] When you sleep, your *Body* goes into recovery mode. Sleep is when your brain and anatomy slow down, repair, and recharge, ensuring you are ready for the next day.[26] Without adequate sleep, these vital recovery processes are compromised. In the short term, a lack of sleep can impair judgment, mood, memory, and the ability to learn. It also increases the risk of accidents and injuries. In the long term, chronic sleep deprivation is linked to serious health problems like obesity, diabetes, heart disease, and even premature death.[27] Research shows that even adding an extra sixty to ninety minutes of sleep per night can improve overall well-being, making us healthier, happier, and safer.[28]

Sleep is clearly essential for maintaining physical health and optimizing your overall best capacity. How are your sleep habits?

Here are some best practices to consider:

- *Quantity*: The American Academy of Sleep Medicine, after reviewing hundreds of research studies, recommends that "healthy adults get at least seven hours of sleep, per night. Babies, young children, and teens require even more sleep to support growth and development."[29]

- *Quality*: Be mindful of your caffeine and alcohol intake, especially in the hours before bed, as both can interfere with sleep.[30] Keep your bedroom quiet, relaxing, and cool. Turn off electronic devices at least thirty minutes before bedtime to reduce disruptions.[31]

- *Routine*: Stick to a consistent sleep schedule, even on weekends. Develop calming bedtime rituals (winding down an hour before bed, turning off screens, or enjoying a cup of herbal tea) to signal to your body that it is time to rest.[32]

By prioritizing the right amount and quality of sleep, you can improve your capacity and overall well-being.

EXERCISE

The World Health Organization reports that "31 percent of the world's adult population, 1.8 billion people, are physically inactive."[33] Despite this, exercise is crucial for health, benefiting nearly every system in your *Body*.

Research in *Comprehensive Physiology* states, "Conclusive evidence exists that physical inactivity is one important cause of most chronic diseases. In addition, physical activity primarily prevents, or delays, chronic diseases, implying that chronic disease need not be an inevitable outcome during life."[34] Studies also show exercise has a positive effect on cognitive health, with physically active adults having a significantly lower risk of cognitive decline and dementia.[35] Moreover, regular physical activity has been linked to improved mood and creativity.[36]

In today's work environment, it is all too easy to be glued to a computer screen all day, whether we are on video calls, answering emails, or managing endless messages. From personal experience, I know how draining it can be. Yet if you want to achieve and sustain your *Elite Energy*, your best capacity, you must prioritize physical movement.

The World Health Organization recommends at least 150 minutes of moderate-intensity physical activity per week.[37] Even just thirty minutes of moderate exercise daily helps meet these guidelines. Harvard Medical School even calls regular exercise "the single most important thing you can do for your health."[38]

If you are feeling burned out, adding physical activity might seem overwhelming, but the key is starting small. As Mark Twain said, "The secret to getting ahead is getting started. The secret of getting started is breaking your complex, overwhelming tasks into small manageable tasks, and then starting on the first one."[39]

Start with small steps and build from there.

- *Set a realistic goal*: Break down your exercise goals into small, manageable tasks. If you are starting from scratch, try adding a twenty-minute walk to your day or make three of your meetings a week walking meetings. If you already have a cardio or strength routine, consider adding stretching once a week. Celebrate the small wins and track your progress.

- *Make it fun*: If you are feeling burned out, choose activities you enjoy. Whether it is dancing, hiking, tennis, or even a pick-up hockey game at lunch, make exercise something you look forward to. This makes it easier to stay motivated.

- *Stay consistent*: Consistency is crucial. Even on days when motivation is low, prioritize movement. You do not always need to do a full workout, sometimes a spontaneous dance break with your kids, a quick walk, or a short stretching session can make a big difference. All movement counts. Keep it regular, and you will feel the benefits over time.

Exercise is a powerful tool for boosting your *Elite Energy*—just start moving.

All of the physical factors we have discussed in this chapter are likely familiar to you, but when we are feeling burned out or overwhelmed, are we actually putting them into practice? Are you truly taking care of your *Body* to support your best capacity, or is this an area of your *Elite Energy* system that is being neglected and could use some attention?

RETURN TO OUR STORY

Let's return to my friend Mark. In 2023, he experienced a wake-up call regarding his health when he had his first ocular migraine. Realizing that his physical health needed to be a priority, for both his well-being and the success of his business, he decided to make significant changes.

Mark adopted a new wellness routine that included limiting alcohol, committing to over fifteen thousand steps a day, drinking 128 ounces of water daily, working out three times a week, using the sauna almost every day, and following a new supplement regimen. Remarkably, within less than a year, he dropped from the 220s to the 170s pounds on the scale. He also managed to reduce his body fat percentage by more than half, currently sitting at around 16 percent.

Even more impactful than the numbers are the changes in his energy levels. "What has been truly remarkable is how quickly my body has transformed by simply introducing new habits," he states. "Not only is my personal health better, but I now have the energy needed to make my business the best it can be."

REFLECT, PROCESS, APPLY

Your turn: Overall we know investing in your *Body*, your physical health and wellness, is critical to obtain and maintain your best capacity and overall well-being. How are you doing right now? If you were to rate your current physical health, your state of being, on a scale of one to ten, how would you rate yourself today?

Self-Rating

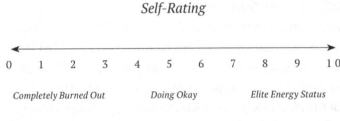

| 0 | 1 | 2 | 3 | 4 | 5 | 6 | 7 | 8 | 9 | 1 0 |

Completely Burned Out   *Doing Okay*   *Elite Energy Status*

Next, how are you doing today in maintaining regular wellness habits and practices that support your physical health and overall well-being?

Self-Assessment

1. I engage in physical activity most days of the week.

   ❏ Yes ❏ No

2. I include a mix of cardiovascular exercise, strength training, and flexibility exercises in my routine.

   ❏ Yes ❏ No

3. I complete at least 150 minutes of moderate-intensity aerobic activity per week.

❏ Yes ❏ No

4. I incorporate movement into my work routine (like walking meetings and taking the stairs).

❏ Yes ❏ No

5. I eat a balanced diet that includes a variety of foods (such as fruits, vegetables, whole grains, lean proteins, and healthy fats).

❏ Yes ❏ No

6. I stay hydrated by drinking plenty of water throughout the day.

❏ Yes ❏ No

7. I maintain a consistent sleep schedule, going to bed and waking up at the same time every day, including weekends.

❏ Yes ❏ No

8. I have a relaxing bedtime routine to help signal to my body that it is time to wind down.

❏ Yes ❏ No

9. My sleep environment is comfortable, dark, quiet, and cool.

❏ Yes ❏ No

10. I limit exposure to screens and electronic devices before bedtime.

❏ Yes ❏ No

Exercise: Start, Stop, Continue

Finally, define and commit to the core habits for your *Elite Energy* system regarding your *Body*, habits to start, stop, or continue. Reflect on the following questions and consider any adjustments you need to make to ensure your physical health is optimized for your best capacity.

1. **Are there any habits or practices regarding my physical wellness that I want to *continue*?**
   Reflect on the positive habits and practices that already support your physical health and help you feel at your best. What are the activities you do regularly that help you maintain your physical vitality?

   Example: "I want to continue my morning stretching routine to improve flexibility and reduce muscle stiffness."

_____

_____

_____

2. **Are there any habits or practices that I should**
   ***stop* to better support my physical health?**
   Identify any habits or activities that might be hindering your physical health, such as poor nutrition, inactivity, or overexertion. What is not benefiting you?

   *Example: "I should stop sitting for long periods without
   moving, as it contributes to back pain and reduces my
   energy levels."*

   _____

   _____

   _____

3. **Are there any habits or practices that I should consider *starting* to better support my physical health?**
   What new physical habits or behaviors could help
   enhance your overall well-being? What changes
   or additions could increase your energy, mobility,
   and long-term health?

   *Example: "I should start incorporating strength
   training into my routine to improve muscle tone and
   increase metabolism."*

   _____

   _____

   _____

4. **Given my assessment, my *number one* commitment for my *Body* is...**

Based on your reflection, identify the most important wellness commitment to your physical health moving forward. What single habit or practice will have the biggest impact on your fitness, energy, and overall well-being?

Example: "My number one commitment is to consistently get at least thirty minutes of moderate exercise every day."

_____

_____

_____

5. **This is my number one commitment because...**

Reflect on why this wellness habit is so important to you. Consider how it will improve your physical health, boost your energy, and enhance your overall well-being.

Example: "Daily exercise is essential because it helps me maintain my energy levels, improves my mood, and keeps me physically strong, which benefits both my personal and professional life."

_____

_____

_____

AN EXAMPLE: BREE'S *ELITE ENERGY*

For my physical wellness assessment, a habit I want to *continue* is my healthy eating. I have always loved whole foods, with lots of fruits and vegetables, and I even try to achieve a large amount of variety of plants each week. One habit I need to *stop*, though, is the tendency to start working whenever I wake up at 3:00 a.m. A habit I want to *start* is a consistent wind-down bedtime routine to help improve my sleep.

However, my number one commitment to my *Elite Energy* system is ensuring I *move* every day. Whether it is yoga, running, or a long walk outside, my goal is to move for at least thirty minutes each day. This simple commitment is a core part of my strategy for better energy, focus, and overall well-being.

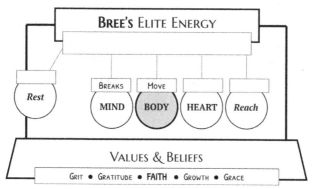

Image 10: Bree's Body Commitment—Move (source: Bree Bacon)

EXCELLENT JOB! YOUR *BODY* COMMITMENT IS NOW SET

Take a moment to write your number one commitment for your *Body* into your *Elite Energy* framework, available to print at www.BreeBacon.com.[40]

By committing to this step, you have made a powerful decision to prioritize your physical health and overall well-being. Now that you have reflected on what works for you, the next step is to integrate these physical habits into your regular routine. You can even encourage others to do the same by sharing your commitment on social media using the hashtag #YourEliteEnergy_Body.

NEXT UP: INVESTING IN YOUR *HEART*

Now that you have defined your commitment for your *Body*, it is time to turn our focus to the last *core* component of your *Elite Energy* system: how to invest in your **Heart**. Take a moment to congratulate yourself for prioritizing your physical wellness—completing part II of III of your *core* for a stronger, more energized version of your *Elite Energy* system.

CHAPTER 7

CORE III—HEART

———

"Our individual relationships are an untapped resource—a source of healing hiding in plain sight."

—Dr. Vivek H. Murthy

My little sister, Amara, could not be more different from me. On the Enneagram chart, she is a four (the individualist), and I am an eight (the challenger). Her StrengthsFinder results include empathy, restorative, developer, individualization, and responsibility. Mine? Focus, learner, achiever, and analytical. Her Myers-Briggs type is ENFJ, the protagonist; mine is ESTJ, the executive.

As young adults, I always found it fascinating how Amara connected with her friends. She would stroll into a coffee shop on a Saturday, casually glance around, and—boom—she was chatting with someone. Me and my friends? We need a carefully coordinated plan with calendar invites sent weeks, if not months, in advance.

Besides her easygoing social nature, Amara stands out for her creativity and her passion for connecting with other like-minded creators. In her free time, she has always been driven to create, whether that is writing and releasing music or even penning a full-length children's movie!

However, when COVID-19 hit, Amara's world changed dramatically. As a single woman, she found herself spending much of the lockdown alone in her apartment, a stark contrast to her usual bustling coffee shop meetups and spontaneous social gatherings. Rather than feeling discouraged, Amara used this time to lean into her creativity and personal growth. She enrolled in a virtual writing course with other creatives and spent countless hours composing new music, which became both a therapeutic outlet and a way to stay connected to other creative minds during a period of isolation.

When restrictions were lifted, Amara's approach to reconnecting with the world was entirely unique. She dove into community theater, an experience that sparked a newfound passion for the performing arts. Not stopping there, she enrolled in improv classes and eventually formed an improv troupe with some of the other adults in her class.

For Amara, relational health and wellness is not just about maintaining relationships; it is about seeking new, vibrant experiences and engaging with others in unexpected, creative ways.

We will circle back to Amara's relational health and wellness journey shortly, but first, let's take a deeper look at the research that shows why taking care of your **Heart**—your relational health and wellness—is essential to fueling your *Elite Energy* system. The *core* of your system relies on more than just your mental and physical health. It is also about nurturing your relationships and seeking meaningful, authentic connections.

CORE III: YOUR HEART

The third element of the *core* of your *Elite Energy* system is your **Heart,** your *relational* health and wellness.

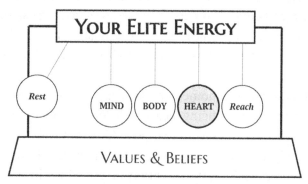

Image 11: Core III: Your Heart (source: Bree Bacon)

Your relational *health* is the structure, function, and quality of your connection to others.[1] *Structure* refers to the number and variety of your relationships (whether with family, friends, colleagues, or neighbors) and how often you interact with them. *Function* relates to how reliable and supportive these relationships are in meeting your various needs. *Quality* speaks to the positive, helpful, and satisfying nature of your interactions and whether they truly nurture you.[2]

Your relational *wellness* involves the ongoing habits and practices that nurture and strengthen your relational health. We will focus our attention here, on how you can consistently cultivate meaningful connections that help you thrive.

WHY IT MATTERS FOR YOUR *ELITE ENERGY*

Did you know people who have friends and close confidants are more satisfied with their lives and less likely to suffer from depression?[3] That with social connections we are less likely to die from all causes, including heart problems and a range of chronic diseases?[4] In fact, research consistently shows that having meaningful relationships is one of the most reliable indicators of a long, healthy, and fulfilling life.[5]

Yet "at any given moment, about one in two of our fellow citizens is experiencing measurable levels of loneliness."[6] In 2023, the United States Surgeon General Vivek Murthy actually declared an epidemic of loneliness and isolation. He sources findings from a variety of disciplines, including epidemiology, neuroscience, medicine, psychology, and sociology, that all come to the same conclusion: Relational health and wellness is a significant predictor of longevity and better physical, cognitive, and mental health, while isolation and loneliness are significant predictors of premature death and poor health.[7]

In the following sections, we will explore some of the key insights Dr. Murthy and his team have outlined, showing how relational health and wellness directly impact your *Elite Energy*.

PHYSICAL HEALTH

Your relational health and wellness are deeply interconnected with the other core elements of your *Elite Energy* system. The state of your relational health directly influences factors like stress hormones, inflammation levels, and even the way your genes are activated and translated into bodily functions.[8]

Research consistently shows that your relational health is closely linked to your physical health. Poor social relationships, isolation, and loneliness increase the risk of coronary heart disease by 29 percent and stroke by 32 percent.[9] Social isolation and less emotional and practical support has also been linked to a higher risk of type 2 diabetes and related complications.[10]

The mortality risks of being socially disconnected are comparable to those of smoking up to fifteen cigarettes a day, and even greater than the risks associated with drinking six or more alcoholic drinks a day.[11] In fact, social isolation can trigger inflammation in the body to levels comparable to those caused by physical inactivity.[12] It also can increase our vulnerability to viruses and respiratory illnesses.[13]

Compelling evidence from 148 studies, with an average follow-up of over seven years, reveals that strong social connections can increase the odds of survival by 50 percent.[14] The National Academies of Sciences Engineering and Medicine *2020 Consensus Study Report* states, "Over four decades of research has produced robust evidence that lacking social connection—and in particular, scoring high on measures of social isolation—is associated with a significantly increased risk for early death from all causes."[15]

MENTAL HEALTH

The state of your relational health and wellness also profoundly influences your mental health. Your social connections shape how you experience stress, manage emotions, and maintain a sense of safety, resilience, and hope.

Research consistently underscores the significance of this connection. When people are socially disconnected, their likelihood of experiencing anxiety and depression increases.[16] Additionally, chronic loneliness and social isolation can increase the risk of developing dementia by up to 50 percent in older adults.[17]

Globally, adults report their relationships with family and close friends are the most important sources of meaning, purpose, and motivation in their lives.[18] These strong social bonds not only enhance emotional health but also improve stress responses, helping to buffer the negative effects of stress on overall well-being.[19]

A recent study highlights the mental health benefits of social support. Participants who gave a speech as part of a stressful task showed significantly lower stress levels when they received positive feedback, underscoring how kindness and encouragement from others can reduce stress and improve emotional health.[20]

YOUR BEHAVIORS

Finally, the state of your relational health profoundly influences your behaviors, including lifestyle choices like diet, exercise, and sleep, as well as health-related behaviors such as taking medication as prescribed or following recommended wellness practices.[21]

Research shows people are more likely to engage in physical activity if their peers and friends also exercise.[22] Similarly, individuals are more likely to quit smoking if their social connections do the same, demonstrating the powerful impact of our social networks on shaping our behaviors.[23]

Social disconnection is linked to reduced productivity in the workplace, poorer academic performance, and lower levels of civic engagement.[24] In the United States, "stress-related absenteeism attributed to loneliness costs employers an estimated $154 billion annually."[25] On the other hand, children and adolescents who have positive relationships with peers, parents, and teachers tend to achieve better academic outcomes.[26] Additionally, participation in community-based activities, like volunteering, has been shown to significantly increase the likelihood of unemployed individuals finding work.[27]

These studies and statistics underscore a critical truth: Investing in your relational health, your social connections, directly impacts your behaviors, physical and mental health, and ultimately, your entire *Elite Energy* system.

RELATIONAL WELLNESS CONSIDERATIONS

Investing in your relational health is crucial, but *how* do you actually go about it? What practical steps can you take to improve your relational health and, in turn, boost your overall *Elite Energy*, your personal best capacity?

Here are a few practices to consider. Keep in mind this is not an exhaustive list but rather a starting point (thought starters, if you will) to help you explore and define the relational wellness habits and practices that will best support your personal *Elite Energy* system and overall well-being.

PUT DOWN YOUR DEVICE

The average American adult spends four to five hours a day on their phone, checking it every four minutes.[28] One in three United States adults aged eighteen and over report being online "almost constantly."[29] In a United States-based study, participants who used social media for more than two hours a day were about twice as likely to report increased feelings of social isolation compared to those who used social media for less than thirty minutes per day.[30]

These statistics highlight how pervasive technology has become in our daily lives, but they also raise important questions about how our digital habits impact our real-world connections and relational health.

When assessing the status of your connections, consider how often your relationships with others are channeled through social media, smartphones, virtual reality, remote work, or other digital technologies. While these advances bring great benefits, it is essential to create enough space in our lives without screens to be more present with one another.

If you feel your devices are getting in the way of deeper connections, start by setting personal goals. Designate technology-free zones or times, like before bed or during meals, and commit to keeping your phone away during social activities so you can focus fully on the people around you. Involve your family or loved ones by creating shared screen-time guidelines, perhaps making the kitchen table a screen-free zone or setting limits on daily screen usage. You can also minimize distractions by using your phone's "silence" or "airplane" mode when you're with others, or even disable app notifications to help you stay present and engaged in the moment.

PRIORITIZE PERSONAL RELATIONSHIPS

Even United States Surgeon General Dr. Vivek Murthy has openly struggled with his own relational health and wellness. After completing his first term as surgeon general, Dr. Murthy found himself disconnected from colleagues he had worked closely with for years. He realized that during his time in office, he had made a critical mistake: He had neglected his personal friendships, convincing himself that he needed to focus entirely on work.[31]

Even when Dr. Murphy was physically present with loved ones, he was not truly there. His mind was often consumed with checking news updates or replying to messages. When his job ended, he felt embarrassed to reach out to those he had ignored and found himself feeling increasingly isolated. This loneliness, much like depression, began to erode his self-esteem and sense of self, leaving him feeling as though he were the only one struggling.[32]

Dr. Murthy is certainly not alone in his struggles. Personally, I also find it challenging to be fully present with my loved ones, especially after a busy workday. I have only a few precious hours each day with my daughter and husband, yet even then, I often find myself distracted, thinking through my to-do list or trying to solve problems from earlier in the day. In fact, as I write this chapter, my three-year-old daughter is trying to crawl into my lap, asking for my attention. (So, excuse me for a moment while I take a quick "mommy monster" play break!)

This brings me to a question for you: Are you truly investing in your personal relationships? Are you spending meaningful time with the people you love and being fully present, or are you constantly caught up in work, responsibilities, and the never-ending demands of your to-do list?

Maybe it is time to act. As stated in the former surgeon general's *Our Epidemic of Loneliness and Isolation*: "Answer that phone call from a friend. Make time to share a meal. Listen without the distraction of your phone. Perform an act of service. Express yourself authentically. The keys to human connection are simple, but extraordinarily powerful."[33]

These actions do not have to be grand gestures. They are simple, intentional steps that can strengthen your connections and make a real difference in your relational health.

ENGAGE IN PROFESSIONAL RELATIONSHIPS

The workplace is not just a place to get things done and earn a paycheck. It is also an opportunity to build meaningful connections. Creating practices and cultivating a culture where people can connect as whole individuals, not just as skill sets, fosters a sense of belonging and teamwork. How are you investing in your professional relationships?

Peers: What habits do you have to connect with your peers, both inside and outside your company? Connecting with people in your industry or field can offer valuable perspectives and insights. These peers often share similar challenges, making it easier to understand one another's experiences. A network of peers provides a supportive space to share concerns, ask for advice, and receive empathy. Consider setting up a monthly breakfast to swap stories, or make it a point to have lunch each Friday with a different colleague or two to learn from their experiences. Walking meetings with coworkers are another great option, offering a more relaxed setting for connection while also allowing you to move your body (a win-win!).

Teams: As we often spend a significant portion of our day working, the quality of our relationships with teammates can directly impact our stress levels, job satisfaction, and overall happiness. What regular habits do you have to connect with your team? Consider setting aside time for regular team-building activities, such as a quarterly book club where you read and discuss a chapter each week, or a monthly in-person training focused on improving collaboration and team dynamics. Even simple practices like doing the *Elite Energy* exercises as a team can help your bond while learning about each other's unique ecosystems.

Mentors: A mentor is someone experienced and trusted who offers guidance, advice, and support over time. Regularly connecting with one or more mentors can be a powerful wellness practice. A good mentor listens attentively, provides valuable feedback, and helps you navigate challenges. They can guide you through decision-making, offer encouragement, and provide constructive feedback to help you grow. If you do not already have a mentor (or two or three), seek someone who genuinely cares about your success and well-being. Make time for monthly coffee dates or quarterly lunches with them. Additionally, you can pay it forward by offering mentorship to others.

EMBRACE COMMUNITY

Community can mean many things, but here I want to focus on your involvement with your local community. Getting involved in local groups can provide regular social contact, offer support, provide a sense of purpose, and help you feel a sense of belonging. Unfortunately, traditional forms of community engagement, such as religious groups, clubs, and labor unions, have been on the decline since the 1970s.[34] In fact, a 2018 report found that only 16 percent of Americans felt very attached to their local community.[35]

Below you will find many ways to change that statistic and build stronger, more connected relationships within your local community.

Participate: One of the simplest ways to improve your social health is by actively participating in local organizations, churches, clubs, or community groups. Whether it is attending a local farmers market, joining a class, or getting involved in a neighborhood event, being a part of local activities can give you the social contact and sense of belonging that benefits your overall well-being. If you cannot find something that suits you, consider starting something yourself. When my husband and I first moved into our home, I wrote a letter to our neighbors asking if anyone wanted to start a book club or wine night. I was amazed when twenty-five neighbors signed up, and we have now been meeting monthly for over five years.

Seek diversity: Expanding your social network to include people of different backgrounds and experiences can have powerful benefits for both you and your community. Engaging with people from diverse walks of life can increase your understanding and help create deeper connections. Studies suggest that having relationships with people who are different from you (not just in terms of culture, but also socioeconomic background or life experience) can boost community health and well-being.[36]

Volunteer: Volunteering is a powerful way to contribute to your community while boosting your own relational health. Research from the *Journal of Happiness Studies* shows that people who volunteer report higher levels of happiness and improved well-being over time.[37] Whether helping at a local library, maintaining public parks, supporting schools, working with charities, or assisting health and wellness programs, volunteering offers tangible benefits for both you and those you serve.

LEAN IN TO CONFLICT RESOLUTION

Conflict is an inevitable part of any relationship, but it does not have to be a reason to walk away. Instead, consider it an opportunity to build stronger connections through empathy, healthy communication, and effective conflict resolution practices.

Cultivating empathy: Empathy involves putting yourself in another person's shoes to understand their perspective, feelings, and experiences. It is essential for strengthening relationships and fostering deeper connections. As Dr. Karina Schumann, a social psychology professor at the University of Pittsburgh, explains, empathy motivates positive behaviors like forgiveness, helping others, and volunteering, while reducing negative behaviors such as aggression and bullying.[38] To practice empathy, engage with people who are different from you, listen actively, and try to understand their viewpoint. Reflect on what might block your empathy, such as assumptions or biases, and work to overcome them.

Communication skills: How you express yourself during conflicts can make or break a relationship. Negative communication styles like criticism (attacking someone's character), contempt (disrespect and disgust), defensiveness (refusing to listen), and stonewalling (withdrawing and avoiding the conversation) can escalate conflicts and damage social health.[39] To improve communication, practice "softening" tough conversations by starting with something positive, appreciating the other person, and tackling one issue at a time. A useful technique is the "speaker-listener" method, where each person takes turns speaking and listening to ensure both parties feel understood.[40] This promotes respectful dialogue and helps prevent misunderstandings.

Healthy resolution: How do you handle conflict? Do you criticize, defend, stonewall, or display contempt? When conflicts arise, emotional and physical stress can cloud our judgment. Taking a break to calm down can help set the stage for a more productive conversation.[41] Practice active listening, ask questions to understand the other person's perspective, and stay open-minded. Question your assumptions, and be willing to admit when you might be wrong. If the conflict is not resolving constructively, consider involving a therapist or mediator to facilitate communication.

A lot of these relational factors may feel familiar, but when we are feeling burned out or overwhelmed, are we actually putting them into practice? Are you truly nurturing your *Heart* to support your best capacity and overall well-being? Is this an area of your *Elite Energy* system that is overlooked and could benefit from more attention?

Taking care of our relationships, whether with our loved ones, our colleagues, or our communities, is essential for our best capacity and overall well-being. If this is a space you have neglected, now might be the time to reassess and give it the care it deserves.

RETURN TO OUR STORY

Now, circling back to my sister Amara. Her journey of discovering new ways to connect during times of isolation can remind all of us just how important it is to nurture our relational wellness in ways that align with our individual personalities and needs. For Amara, that means constantly seeking new creative outlets, embracing spontaneity, and engaging with others in ways that spark her joy.

As she puts it, "I've realized that when my work tank is empty, it's often because I'm lacking creative and social stimulation in my personal life. Creative experiences are the fuel for my brain. If I'm not having spontaneous, interesting interactions with others, my ability to stay energized at work starts to fade."

Amara's approach to relational wellness serves as a reminder that we all need to take an intentional, personal approach to building relationships. When you do, you activate a powerful driver of your best capacity and overall well-being.

REFLECT, PROCESS, APPLY

Your turn: Overall we know investing in your *Heart*, your relational health and wellness, is critical to obtaining and maintaining your best capacity. How are you doing right now? If you were to rate your current relational health, your state of being, on a scale of one to ten, how would you rate yourself today?

Self-Rating

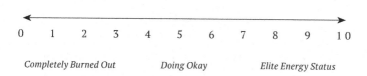

Next, how are you doing today in maintaining regular wellness habits and practices that support your relational health and overall *Elite Energy* system?

Self-Assessment

1. I am satisfied with the *quantity* of my relationships: family, friends, and community.

   ❏ Yes ❏ No

2. I am satisfied with the *quality* of my relationships: family, friends, and community.

   ❏ Yes ❏ No

3. I have a supportive social network I can rely on in times of need.

   ❏ Yes ❏ No

4. I belong to community or social groups outside of work.

❏ Yes ❏ No

5. I regularly engage in meaningful social activities that bring me joy.

❏ Yes ❏ No

6. I engage in social activities that foster a sense of community and belonging.

❏ Yes ❏ No

7. I communicate respectfully and effectively with others.

❏ Yes ❏ No

8. I have open and honest conversations with people close to me.

❏ Yes ❏ No

9. I am equipped to manage and resolve interpersonal conflicts effectively.

❏ Yes ❏ No

10. I seek out new social experiences or challenges.

❏ Yes ❏ No

Exercise: Start, Stop, Continue

Now, define and commit to the core habits for your *Elite Energy* system regarding your *Heart*, your relational health. Reflect on the following questions to identify practices that nurture your connections with others, ensuring that your relational wellness is optimized for sustained energy and overall well-being.

1. **Are there any habits or practices regarding my relational wellness I want to *continue*?**
Reflect on the positive habits and practices that already support your relational health, that help you feel at your best. What activities or behaviors do you engage in that help foster strong, meaningful connections with others?

   Example: "I want to continue having regular social dates with close friends to stay connected and offer support."

   _____

   _____

   _____

2. **Are there any habits or practices I should *stop* to better support my relational health?**
Identify any habits or behaviors that might be hindering your ability to connect with others, for example, poor communication, neglecting relationships, or emotional distancing. What is not benefiting your relational health?

Example: "I should stop canceling plans last minute due to work, as it strains relationships and makes me feel disconnected."

_____

_____

_____

3. **Are there any habits or practices I should consider *starting* to better support my relational health?**
What new behaviors or actions could help enhance your relational health? Consider any changes or additions that could deepen your relationships, build emotional intimacy, and foster connection.

Example: "I should start setting aside time each week for a family activity to strengthen our bond and create new memories."

_____

_____

_____

4. **Given my assessment, my *number one* commitment for my *Heart* is...**
Based on your reflection, identify the most important wellness commitment for your relational health moving forward. What single habit or practice will

have the biggest impact on the quality of your connections and overall well-being?

Example: *"My number one commitment is to prioritize quality time with my partner, even if it is just fifteen minutes a day without distractions."*

_____

_____

_____

5. **This is my number one commitment because...**
Reflect on why this wellness habit is so important to you. Consider how it will improve your relational health, boost your energy, and enhance your overall well-being.

Example: *"Spending uninterrupted time with my partner is essential because it deepens our connection, reduces stress, and helps me feel more supported in both my personal and professional life."*

_____

_____

_____

AN EXAMPLE: BREE'S *ELITE ENERGY*

For my personal assessment, a habit I want to *continue* is putting away technology during meals. My husband and I decided to make it a family rule that no work emails, social media, or screens would be allowed at the dinner table. Mealtime is for connecting as a family, and that simple change has made a significant difference.

A habit I want to *stop* is avoiding conflict. I will be honest, I hate conflict. When I sense tension or disagreement, my first instinct is to retreat. However, avoiding conflict is obviously not healthy for my relationships or my overall well-being. I have realized that learning how to address and resolve conflict is essential for maintaining strong, authentic connections, so it is something I am actively working on.

A habit I want to *start* is volunteering with the children's ministries at my church. It is a meaningful way to give back to my community while also spending quality time with my daughter, a win-win that nurtures both my relational wellness and gives me a sense of fulfillment through service.

My number one commitment for my *Heart*, my relational health and wellness, is to *be present* with my family. Even when I am physically present with my husband Neil and daughter Eliana, I often find my mind wandering to solve whatever problem the day brought. It is easy to get distracted, even when technology is put away. My husband and daughter are my most important relationships, and being truly present with them—emotionally, mentally, and physically—is my number one commitment for them and for my own relational health and overall *Elite Energy* system.

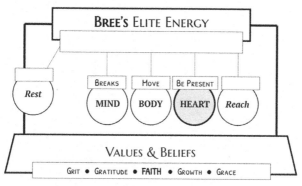

Image 12: Bree's Heart Commitment—
Be Present (source: Bree Bacon)

NICE WORK! YOUR *HEART* COMMITMENT IS NOW SET

Take a moment to write your number one commitment for your *Heart* into your *Elite Energy* framework, available to print at www.BreeBacon.com.[42]

By committing to this step, you have made a powerful decision to prioritize your relational health and overall well-being. Now that you have reflected on what works for you, the next step is to integrate these relationship habits into your regular routine. You can even encourage others to do the same by sharing your commitment on social media using the hashtag #YourEliteEnergy_Heart.

NEXT UP: BALANCING *REACH* AND *REST*

Now that you have defined your commitment for your *Heart*, it is time to turn our focus to how to **Rest**, or recharge, and when to **Reach** or challenge yourself. Take a moment to congratulate yourself for completing the *core* of your system: *Mind, Body* and *Heart*!

CHAPTER 8

REST AND REACH

---

*"Humans are these rhythms of contracting
and releasing, inhaling and exhaling,
without which we cannot exist."*

—KIMERER LAMOTHE

In today's culture, we are told to hustle harder, work longer, and never stop pushing ourselves. The messages are everywhere, whether it is in the constant pursuit of career growth, the pressure to achieve personal goals, or the idolization of "busy." Yet, if you want to obtain and maintain your *Elite Energy*, your best capacity, endless pushing is not the answer.

The real secret is in balance. It is the rhythm of **Rest** and **Reach**. It is about knowing when to challenge yourself and when to step back, allowing your *Mind*, *Body*, and *Heart* the space they need to recover and recharge. This balance is not just a nice-to-have. It is essential for your best capacity; your energy, creativity, effectiveness, and overall well-being.

Consider your *Body* and exercise. Intense workouts create tiny tears in your muscles. Without rest, those muscles cannot repair, which can lead to overtraining syndrome— fatigue, dehydration, and mood disturbances. When you *Rest* properly, your *Body* has time to heal and grow stronger, improving your performance.[1] *Rest* is not just recovery; it is a crucial part of progress. Without it, your *Body* cannot reach its full potential.

Similarly, if you are facing a tough problem, research shows that stepping back and sleeping on it can make you twice as likely to solve it.[2] When experimenting with new ideas, research shows that taking time to relax can actually boost your creativity. Letting in some sunshine, finding moments of joy, and allowing your mind to wander without pressure often lead to the most innovative breakthroughs.[3] *Rest* is not just a pause; it is a key driver of insight and creativity.

In an article for *Psychology Today*, Kimerer LaMothe, a philosopher, dancer, and scholar, delves into the inherent rhythms that sustain our lives.[4] She reflects on how our survival depends not just on the presence of vital organs but on their ability to function in rhythmic, alternating cycles. Specifically, she notes the heart and lungs must work in harmony—our heart contracting and releasing, our lungs inflating and deflating— repeatedly, 24-7. These rhythms are essential to our very existence.[5]

In every area of life, the key is finding the balance between pushing yourself to *Reach* new heights and allowing time to *Rest* and recharge. When you strike this balance, you not only tap into your best capacity but also maintain your overall well-being and vitality over the long term.

Rest fuels your *Reach*, and *Reach* energizes your *Rest*. Together, they create a dynamic rhythm that sustains your energy and vitality. Much like the body's natural rhythms of contraction and release, our energy systems thrive when we alternate between challenging ourselves and giving ourselves time to recover.

In your own *Elite Energy* system, you have set your foundational *Values & Beliefs*. You have made regular wellness commitments to support your *Mind, Body*, and *Heart*—your mental, physical, and relational health. However, for your system to truly thrive, it is not enough to focus solely on your core commitments. You must also allow time to contract and time to release, time to inflate and time to deflate—time to *Rest* and time to *Reach*.

FINDING BALANCE: *REST* AND *REACH*
Rest involves practices that help us relax, unwind, and recharge. It can take many forms: taking a break from stress to let your *Mind* rejuvenate; allowing your *Body* the time it needs to recover and rebuild; connecting with loved ones or engaging in social activities that nourish your *Heart*; or nurturing your *Values & Beliefs* through journaling, quiet retreats, or inspirational reading.

Ultimately, *Rest* creates moments of tranquility that allow for renewal and recuperation, providing the necessary space for restoration.

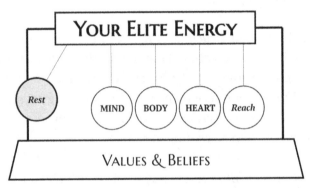

Image 13: Rest (source: Bree Bacon)

Reach is about challenging yourself to grow, learn, and expand your limits. It involves stepping outside your comfort zone to pursue new experiences and take on tasks that push you beyond what is familiar. This could mean learning a new skill, tackling a different type of workout, or taking on a new project at work. It might involve joining a new community group, volunteering for a cause you care about, or signing up for a challenge like a race or a thirty-day commitment.

By taking on new challenges—whether you succeed or fail—you build resilience, acquire new insights, and grow your confidence.

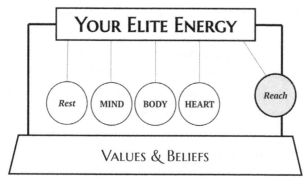

Image 14: Reach (source: Bree Bacon)

The key between these two ends of the pendulum is *balance*.

By alternating between periods of restoration and moments of challenge, we can maintain our well-being while ensuring our best capacity. Both are essential; *Rest* rejuvenates us, and *Reach* extends our capacity.

Together, they create a sustainable rhythm for our best, most energized lives.

WHY IT MATTERS FOR YOUR *ELITE ENERGY*

Your *Elite Energy* system is designed around Newton's pendulum for a reason. For the pendulum to function effectively, every component must be in balance and work in harmony.

We will further explore the concept of balance between the components in chapter 10, but let's recall the pendulum analogy from chapter 3. When you pull the end ball (*Rest*) away and release it, it strikes the middle balls, transmitting energy through the core (*Mind*, *Body*, and *Heart*), ultimately pushing the opposite end ball (*Reach*) into the air. That ball then swings back, repeating the process in the opposite direction. This creates a rhythm, with the two end balls taking turns rising into the air and striking the middle balls. You do not get the smooth, efficient clicking rhythm of the pendulum without both end balls taking their turns.

The same holds true for *Rest* and *Reach*.

You cannot challenge yourself all the time, constantly pushing beyond your limits, and expect to function at your best. Your system needs *Rest*. It needs to recover, rebuild, and replenish.

In a world where busyness is often celebrated, we tend to forget the power of slowing down. However, downtime is essential for our best capacity, as it helps reset your nervous system. Taking time to *Rest* improves your mood, increases productivity, enhances your health, and ultimately leads to greater happiness.[6]

As psychologist Scott Bea from the Cleveland Clinic explains, "So many of us define ourselves by what we do. So we overdo, overwork, and overproduce."[7] He further adds that in our culture, "downtime" is often seen as a weakness. Yet Dr. Bea emphasizes the vital role *Rest* plays: "Our brains are like sponges. They can only soak up so much information before they're saturated, then they have to dry out a bit."[8] Your brain needs *Rest*.

I had the opportunity to chat with Dr. Jerome M. Adams, the twentieth surgeon general of the United States, about the *Elite Energy* concept. We were discussing how society often embraces a "pull yourself up by your bootstraps" mentality, expecting us to constantly push ourselves. I shared, "Yeah, and I pushed myself so hard I landed straight in the hospital. We are not machines!"

Dr. Adams responded, "Not only are we not machines, we treat ourselves worse than machines. We inherently know that machines need rest. Take a car, for example. We know it needs regular oil changes and tire rotations, and we understand that in the summer, you can't run it too long or it overheats, and in the winter, it needs time to warm up. We know you can't run the engine constantly. We are so much more valuable than machines, yet we don't treat ourselves with even that same level of respect and care."

While society often overemphasizes the importance of *Reach*, constantly pushing ourselves beyond our limits, it is equally crucial to recognize that resting too much can also hinder performance. Your *Elite Energy* systems require both *Rest* and *Reach*.

To operate at your best capacity, stepping outside your comfort zone and embracing challenges is also essential. By facing both success and failure, you grow, push the boundaries of what you thought possible, and develop new skills. Expanding your knowledge and capabilities helps you navigate obstacles, adapt, and build resilience.

"You may have heard of 'fixed' and 'growth' mindsets," concepts introduced by Stanford researcher Carol Dweck.[9] A fixed mindset views abilities as static, leading individuals to avoid mistakes for fear they will hinder future success. In contrast, a growth mindset sees change and setbacks as opportunities to learn and improve. By stepping outside your comfort zone, embracing both success and failure, and learning from each, you expand your capabilities, build resilience, and push the boundaries of what you can achieve.[10]

The importance of growth is so fundamental to our well-being that the United States Surgeon General's 2022 report lists opportunities for learning and growth as one of the five essentials for workplace mental health and well-being. It states, "This essential rests on the human needs of learning and accomplishment [...] when organizations create more opportunities for learning, accomplishment, and growth, workers become more optimistic about their abilities and more enthusiastic about contributing to the organization."[11]

A study conducted by researchers at the Wharton School and the Anderson School of Management underscores the critical need for both *Rest* and *Reach* for your *Elite Energy* system. By analyzing two large-scale data sets involving 35,375 Americans and conducting two experiments, they explored how discretionary time affects well-being. They found that too little rest led to lower well-being due to stress, while too much rest resulted in a decline in well-being, driven by a lack of personal growth and challenge.[12]

In case I have not driven the point home enough yet, the key takeaway is *balance*. Your *Elite Energy* system thrives when both *Rest* and *Reach* work together in harmony.

REST AND *REACH* CONSIDERATIONS

We know balance is essential between *Rest* and *Reach*, but how can you put this balance into practice?

To help guide you, I have provided some thought starters broken down by the components of your *Elite Energy* system: *Values & Beliefs, Mind, Body,* and *Heart.* I have not specifically marked what counts as *Rest* versus *Reach* because what might be restful for one person can be a stretch for another.

For example, gardening might be deeply relaxing for one person but a stretch goal for someone else. A night out with friends could be restorative for me, but for my introverted husband, it is a challenge. Your *Elite Energy* system is a personal framework, and it is up to you to identify what restores you (*Rest*) and what challenges you (*Reach*).

As you go through this list, reflect on what activities you find restful versus those you see as a challenge, or perhaps neither. Feel free to brainstorm additional activities you personally find restful or stretching in each area of your *Elite Energy* system.

Values & Beliefs (Your Foundation):

- Set aside thirty minutes each day for quiet reflection.
- Schedule mindfulness meditations at key points during your day.
- Take a few minutes each day to focus on your breath and observe your thoughts.

- Journal daily about how your actions align with your *Values & Beliefs.*
- Attend a retreat or workshop to deepen your understanding of your beliefs.
- Engage in open-minded conversations with those who hold different beliefs or values.
- Seek diverse perspectives that challenge or expand your worldview.
- Write down three things you are thankful for every day.
- Read or listen to new materials about your philosophies or values.
- Take a break from your usual environment to reflect in a new setting.
- Seek mentorship from someone who embodies the values you admire.

Mind (Core I):

- Pick up a new skill or hobby (such as a musical instrument, painting, or cooking).
- Indulge in a book or magazine that piques your interest.
- Challenge yourself to read a book on an unfamiliar topic.
- Treat yourself to a luxurious bath or spa day at home.
- Engage in coloring or drawing as a relaxing creative outlet.
- Spend time journaling or reflecting on your thoughts and feelings.
- Enroll in courses or workshops on topics that spark your curiosity.

- Start a blog or write essays experimenting with new styles or genres.
- Pursue further education or certifications in an area of interest.
- Create a weekly "mental workout" routine (like puzzles or brain games).
- Immerse yourself in a documentary or podcast on a new subject.
- Start a creative project that involves both learning and making.

Body (Core II):

- Spend time outdoors with activities like hiking, kayaking, or skiing.
- Practice yoga, Pilates, or regular stretching routines.
- Set a specific fitness goal like running, weightlifting, or endurance.
- Try a new sport like rock climbing, martial arts, or dance.
- Sign up for a fitness event like a 5K, obstacle course, or cycling tour.
- Switch up your workout routine for thirty days or more.
- Add strength training, cardio, or HIIT to your fitness plan.
- Join a fitness or nutrition challenge, online or in person.
- Incorporate mindful movement like a walking meditation.
- Explore nature through hikes, beach walks, or forest trails.

- Commit to *Body* resets like massages, therapy, or sauna sessions.
- Schedule check-ins with a coach or personal trainer for accountability.
- Prioritize recovery with foam rolling, stretching, or cold therapy.
- Experiment with new nutrition plans or try a new healthy recipe once a week.

Heart (Core III):

- Take a break from screens to reconnect with loved ones in real time.
- Join a book club or an online discussion group to engage with new ideas.
- Attend social events, community gatherings, or local meetups.
- Reconnect with colleagues, neighbors, or old friends.
- Practice active listening to understand others' perspectives and deepen empathy.
- Start conversations with unfamiliar people or acquaintances.
- Volunteer for a cause you care about to make a meaningful impact.
- Plan regular meetups with close friends or family to nurture relationships.
- Attend intimate gatherings with a select group instead of large social events.
- Offer support through small acts of kindness to brighten someone's day.
- Engage in meaningful one-on-one conversations with loved ones to build connection.

- Send handwritten notes or thoughtful messages to show appreciation for others.
- Create or join a close-knit support group or community.

Remember, *Rest* and *Reach* are personal and can look different for everyone. It is important to explore various activities and find what truly works for you. The key is to prioritize and make time for what nourishes your *Values & Beliefs, Body, Mind*, and *Heart*, ensuring you have the space to refresh and recharge. At the same time, ensure you also set reasonable new challenges for yourself to keep growing and learning.

By balancing your need for both *Rest* and *Reach*, you unlock, sustain, and grow your best capacity.

REFLECT, PROCESS, APPLY
Your turn: Balancing *Reach* and *Rest* is essential for your *Elite Energy* to ensure you are thriving, not just surviving. How are you doing right now?

If you were to rate your *balance* of *Rest* and *Reach* on a scale from one to ten, where would you place yourself today?

Self-Rating

Next, how are you doing today maintaining regular habits and practices to support your need for both *Rest* and *Reach*?

Self-Assessment

1. I set boundaries around work hours and personal time to ensure a healthy balance.

❏ Yes ❏ No

2. I allow myself to fully disconnect from work during periods of *Rest*.

❏ Yes ❏ No

3. I make time for activities that bring me joy and relaxation, such as hobbies, exercise, or spending time with loved ones.

❏ Yes ❏ No

4. I recognize the signs I need *Rest* and take proactive steps, such as delegating tasks, seeking support, or taking time off when needed.

❏ Yes ❏ No

5. I regularly assess my workload and commitments to ensure they align with my values and priorities, adjusting as needed to prevent being overwhelmed.

❏ Yes ❏ No

6. I embrace failure as an opportunity to learn and grow.

❏ Yes ❏ No

7. I set goals that push me beyond my comfort zone.

❏ Yes ❏ No

8. I seek out new experiences or learning opportunities.

❏ Yes ❏ No

9. I take on stretch projects or tasks that make me a little nervous or intimidate me.

❏ Yes ❏ No

10. I balance taking risks with maintaining my overall well-being.

❏ Yes ❏ No

Exercise: Start, Stop, Continue

Finally, define and commit to the central habits for your *Elite Energy* system regarding how you *Rest* and *Reach*. This is your personal framework, so consider what works best for you.

1. **Are there any habits or practices regarding how I *Rest* and *Reach* I want to *continue*?**
   Reflect on the practices or routines that currently support your balance of *Rest* and *Reach*. Which

habits help you recharge, and which ones stretch you in positive ways?

Example: "I want to continue taking ten-minute mindfulness breaks during the workday to recharge my mental energy."

_____

_____

_____

2. **Are there any habits or practices I should *stop* to better support how I *Rest* and how I *Reach*?** Identify any habits or routines currently depleting your energy, hindering your ability to rest effectively, or preventing you from reaching your potential. What can you eliminate to improve your overall well-being?

Example: "I should stop saying yes to every request or opportunity without considering my current workload or energy levels. Moving forward, I will sleep on it and take time to assess whether it aligns with my priorities before committing."

_____

_____

_____

3. **Are there any habits or practices I should consider** *starting* **to better support how I** *Rest* **and how I** *Reach*?
Think about new actions or behaviors that could enhance your ability to recharge or challenge yourself. What can you incorporate into your routine to optimize both recovery and growth?

Example: "I should start setting a monthly goal to step outside my comfort zone, like attending a networking event or taking a new class."

_____

_____

_____

4. **Given my assessment, my** *number one* **commitment for how I will** *Rest* **is...**
From your reflection, define your top commitment to *Rest*. This practice or habit will have the greatest positive impact on your well-being and ability to recharge.

Example: "My number one commitment is to prioritize thirty minutes of quiet time every morning before I start my day."

_____

_____

_____

5. **This is my number one *Rest* commitment because...**
Reflect on why this commitment is so important. How will this habit help you recharge, maintain your energy levels, and create a sustainable balance between *Rest* and *Reach*?

Example: "Having thirty minutes of quiet time allows me to center myself, clear my mind, and start my day with focus, which improves my overall energy and productivity."

_____

_____

_____

6. **My current *number one Reach* goal is...**
Based on your current priorities, identify your primary goal for growth or challenge. This is the stretch goal that will push you to reach higher, expand your capabilities, and build resilience.

Example: "My number one Reach goal is to complete a 10K race in the next six months."

_____

_____

_____

7. **This is my current *Reach* goal because...**
Reflect on why this goal is important to you. How will achieving this challenge help you expand your capabilities, build resilience, and boost your overall energy?

Example: "This goal will push me to improve my physical fitness, boost my confidence, and create a sense of accomplishment that drives me to take on other challenges."

_____

_____

_____

AN EXAMPLE: BREE'S *ELITE ENERGY*

When I assess my *Rest*, I recognized some habits I need to *stop*, like scrolling on my phone during breaks. If anything, it causes more anxiety than relaxation. I also see some new practices to *start*, such as incorporating more stretching into my day and spending time hiking in nature or gardening. However, my number one commitment for *Rest* is setting aside one full day a week with no work. This twenty-four-hour period is a time where I will not check my work email, and instead I engage in activities that nourish me, like volunteering with my daughter's class at church, reading a book, or even taking a nap.

For *Reach*, I recognized I often challenge myself *too* much by taking on multiple projects at once, especially with work. While I thrive on challenges, I tend to overcommit, which eventually drains my energy. To address this, I decided to *start* choosing just one personal challenge at a time. For me, that challenge right now is writing and launching this book! Now that it is launched, I plan to let my *Elite Energy* pendulum swing back toward *Rest* for a while. When I feel restored and ready, I will set my next *Reach* goal.

What will it be? Stay tuned...

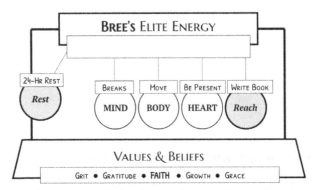

Image 15: Bree's Rest & Reach Commitments (source: Bree Bacon)

CONGRATULATIONS! YOUR *REST* AND *REACH* COMMITMENTS ARE SET

Take a moment to write your number one commitment for *Rest* and *Reach* into your *Elite Energy* framework, available to print at www.BreeBacon.com.[13]

By committing to these steps, you have made a powerful decision to optimize your energy and well-being by balancing how you recharge and when you challenge yourself. Reflecting on what works for you is key, and now it is time to integrate these practices into your routine.

Remember, you do not have to go it alone. Share your commitment with others and inspire them to do the same by using the hashtags #YourEliteEnergy_Rest or #YourEliteEnergy_Reach.

NEXT UP: PURPOSE STATEMENT

Now that you have set your current commitments for *Rest* and *Reach*, we are going to discuss an option to add your personal *Purpose Statement*. This is the final step in solidifying your *Elite Energy* framework.

Take a moment to celebrate your progress. By establishing your *Values & Beliefs, Mind, Body, Heart, Rest*, and *Reach*, you have built a powerful system to sustain and amplify your best capacity and overall well-being.

CHAPTER 9

PURPOSE STATEMENT

———

"The two most important days in life are the day you were born and the day you discover the reason why."

—MARK TWAIN

Here is a bold assertion: If you are feeling burned out, completely exhausted, or have already crashed and burned (like I did), do not start with your purpose. I know, it might sound contradictory to most advice out there, but stick with me. I will explain why shortly.

At this point, you have outlined your personal *Elite Energy* system: your foundational *Values & Beliefs*; the core wellness practices for your *Mind*, *Body*, and *Heart*; and identified the ways you *Rest* and *Reach*. If you are ready for the next step, this is where you can craft your **Purpose Statement**, your personal "why."

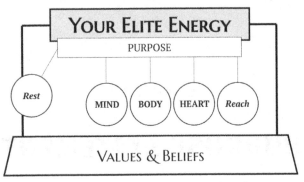

Image 16: Purpose Statement (source: Bree Bacon)

Your purpose is not just a personal goal; it is your connection to something larger than yourself. It is an intention or mission deeply meaningful to you and, ideally, leaves a positive imprint on the world. The reason you commit to your *Elite Energy* system, it is the driving force behind *why* you choose to invest in your best capacity.

Defining your "why" is what will give your *Elite Energy* system focus, clarity, and a sense of direction. It is a statement that ties everything together, anchoring your efforts with a sense of deeper meaning.

WHY IT MATTERS FOR YOUR *ELITE ENERGY*

When you have a well-defined "why" in your life, it provides more than just direction and motivation; it gives you a lens for navigating both your daily choices and life's inevitable challenges. This clarity sparks your passion, fortifies your determination, and nourishes your sense of meaning and fulfillment. Even more importantly, it is a source of resilience when times get tough.

Besides direction and focus, scientific evidence increasingly points to the fact that a deep sense of purpose is linked to better physical and mental health, and even longer life. In 2017, a study from the Harvard School of Public Health found that individuals who report having a greater sense of purpose tend to maintain better health and greater physical vitality as they age.[1] Moreover, research has consistently shown that a well-defined purpose helps lower stress, reduces symptoms of depression and anxiety, and enhances overall resilience to life's setbacks.[2]

Studies also show that people with a clear sense of purpose tend to enjoy better sleep, have stronger immune systems, and experience sharper cognitive function.[3] In 2022, a health and retirement study involving over twelve thousand participants analyzed whether positive changes in purpose correlated with better health outcomes. The results were striking: Those with the highest levels of purpose had a 46 percent lower risk of mortality, 13 percent lower risk of sleep issues, and greater optimism. Additionally, they had a 43 percent lower risk of depression and reported less loneliness.[4]

Purpose, it turns out, influences the *Mind*, *Body*, and *Heart*.

Further supporting the life-enhancing benefits of purpose, a 2023 study by the American Psychological Association found that workers who reported having meaningful work experienced significantly lower stress levels. Only 45 percent of those with meaningful work reported feeling tense or stressed during the workday, compared to a whopping 71 percent of those who felt disconnected from the meaning of their work.[5]

Professor Victor Strecher, author of *Life on Purpose* and a researcher dedicated to understanding what makes life truly meaningful, offers a thought-provoking analogy to highlight the profound impact of purpose. He writes:

> So let's imagine a drug that was shown to add years to your life; reduce the risk of heart attack and stroke; cut your risk of Alzheimer's disease by more than half; help you relax during the day and sleep better at night; double your chances of staying drug- and alcohol-free after treatment; activate your natural killer cells; diminish your inflammatory cells; increase your good cholesterol; and repair your DNA. What if this imaginary drug reduced hospital stays so much that it put a dent in the national health-care crisis? Oh, and as a bonus, gave you better sex? The pharmaceutical company who made the drug would be worth billions. The inventors of the drug would receive Nobel Prizes and have institutes named for them! But it's not a drug. It's purpose. And it's free.[6]

WHY IS THIS LAST?

If purpose is as vital as we have discussed, why does it come at the end of your *Elite Energy* system instead of at the beginning?

The answer is simple: Discovering your purpose is a journey. To fully embrace that journey and uncover your unique impact, you must first be in a place of health and balance.

When I hit rock bottom, I struggled deeply with my sense of purpose. *Why was I working so hard? What was it all for? What kind of impact was I truly making in the world?*

These questions can feel overwhelming when you are not in a healthy state. If you are not sleeping well; if your *Mind* is in a rough spot; if you are neglecting your *Body*; or if your foundational *Values & Beliefs* are unclear, then pressuring yourself to define your purpose is the wrong order of operations.

Before you can truly focus on purpose, you need to take care of your overall ecosystem. You need to prioritize getting healthy: *Mind*, *Body*, and *Heart*. Reconnect with your *Values & Beliefs* and give yourself permission to *Rest* and recharge. Maybe take a moment to define some personal goals or simply allow yourself the grace to take things slow. It is perfectly okay not to have a clearly defined purpose right now.

The important thing to remember is: You do not need to accomplish anything to have value.

Your worth is not defined by your productivity or the grandness of your impact. The world does not need you to "achieve" anything to matter. Your worth is not tied to your next goal, your next accomplishment, or your next big move.

You are valuable because you are *you*, because you bring a unique energy—a distinct capacity—to the world that no one else can replicate.

Take the pressure off yourself to figure it all out. Whether or not you have a purpose statement, whether you are in the middle of a career shift or just beginning to reflect on your path, you matter right now. It is okay not to have everything figured out. It is all right to *Rest*; to pause, reflect, and give yourself the space to figure out who you want to be and what potential impact you want to make.

Each person's journey toward purpose is deeply personal. It requires time, exploration, and the openness to learn from both your successes and your failures. As you navigate through different paths, you are constantly growing, evolving, and refining your understanding of what truly resonates with you and what kind of difference you can uniquely make.

In the meantime, embrace the journey with the courage to explore, question, and learn. Trust that your purpose will reveal itself when the time is right, and that it will be as unique and extraordinary as you are.

THE STRUCTURE OF A PURPOSE STATEMENT

A strong purpose statement is clear, concise, and action-oriented. It answers questions like: *What impact do I want to make? Why does it matter? How will I make it happen?* It is best kept concise, ideally no longer than one or two sentences. The clearer and more focused it is, the more powerful it becomes.

When crafting your statement, focus on three essential components:

- *Desired impact*: What change or outcome do you want to create? What result are you targeting with your efforts?
- *Who you will impact*: What people, groups, or communities do you want to reach or influence?
- *Action or approach*: How will you make it happen? What actions, skills, or talents will you use to achieve your goal?

By combining these three components, you create a purposeful and motivating statement. While your statement can take various forms, below is an example structure to guide you:

To (desired impact), for (who you will impact), using (actions or skills).

To help inspire you, here are some examples of how these three components can come to life in a purpose statement.

- To teach young leaders to become confident, compassionate individuals.
- To inspire young adults to embrace their creativity through art.
- To provide mental health support to veterans through accessible resources.
- To develop technologies that enhance health care access for rural communities.
- To create high school educational content that makes complex ideas accessible.

- To craft experiences that foster human connection among elderly communities.
- To drive environmental sustainability by promoting eco-friendly practices in organizations.

These examples illustrate how a focused impact, a clear audience, and specific actions can form the foundation of a strong, motivating purpose statement.

Remember, your purpose can be a living, evolving concept. As you grow and experience new things, your purpose might shift or expand, and that is okay. Be flexible and let it evolve, but always stay grounded in what truly matters to you. A powerful purpose statement is not just something you write. It is something that fuels you, gives you focus, and keeps you inspired.

REFLECT, PROCESS, APPLY

Your turn: If you already have a purpose statement, take a moment to write it down and reflect on the questions below. Does your purpose still resonate with you? Is there anything you would like to adjust or refine?

If you do not have a purpose statement yet, use the following questions to help you reflect on what might be your "why" and begin to shape your purpose.

1. **What are your foundational values and beliefs?** Reflect on the foundation you identified in chapter 4 that shapes how you live and make decisions.

Example: If you value sustainability and environmental responsibility, your purpose might involve working in conservation, promoting green business practices, or educating others on reducing their environmental footprint.

_____

_____

_____

2. What activities bring you joy and fulfillment?

Think about the activities or experiences that make you feel alive, energized, and at peace.

Example: If you feel most alive when you are creating something tangible, like painting, writing, or designing, your purpose could be to inspire others with your creativity, whether through art, design, or storytelling.

_____

_____

_____

3. What inspires you to grow and push your limits?

Consider the people, stories, or experiences that motivate you to be your best.

Example: If you are inspired by leaders who advocate for mental health, your purpose could involve

supporting others through therapy, community pro-
grams, or creating resources to raise awareness.

_____

_____

_____

4. What are your strengths and talents?
Identify qualities or skills that you naturally excel at or others recognize in you.

Example: If you are a natural communicator with the ability to explain complex ideas in simple ways, your purpose could involve educating others, whether through teaching, writing, or public speaking.

_____

_____

_____

5. What challenges or needs do you feel passionate about addressing?
Reflect on the issues in the world that resonate most with you.

Example: If you are passionate about helping under-served populations, your purpose could involve working with non-profits to provide resources for

low-income communities or advocating for policy
changes to improve access to health care or education.

_____

_____

_____

Ready to write your personal purpose statement?

Before you begin drafting, take a moment to revisit the key questions and the structure that will guide your purpose statement. Answer the following:

1. **Desired impact**: What change or outcome do I want to create? What result am I aiming for with my efforts?

_____

_____

2. **Who you will impact**: Who are the people, groups, or communities I want to reach or influence?

_____

_____

3. **Action or approach**: How will I make it happen? What actions, skills, or talents will I use to achieve this goal?

_____

_____

Write down your proposed purpose statement. Remember, the key is to keep it clear, concise, and motivating. If you need a structure, you have the option to leverage the following:

To (desired impact), for (who you will impact), using (actions or skills).

_____

_____

_____

Once you have a draft of your purpose statement, take some time to let it sit and reflect on it. Do not rush to make it perfect right away. Allow it to evolve and shift as you gain more clarity on what truly matters to you. Your purpose is a dynamic, ongoing process, so give yourself the grace to refine it over time.

AN EXAMPLE: BREE'S *ELITE ENERGY*

For much of my life, I have been really good at following a plan laid out for me. Tell me how to get an A, and I will strive for it 110 percent. Many of the opportunities in my career came because someone recognized my strengths and invited me to join a project or organization. Aside from deciding to pursue a master's in business administration (MBA) in my early twenties, defining what I truly wanted to do and the impact I wanted to make has always been elusive. Even when I was writing my MBA entrance essays, I struggled with the "what's next" question.

Now in my forties, I have had experiences, struggles, successes, and failures that have all led me to help discover what I believe my unique impact is supposed to be. Pondering on the "Reflect, Process, Apply" questions, along with the key questions for crafting a purpose statement—*What's my desired impact? Who do I want to impact? And how will I do it?*—my "why" became clear.

My purpose is to be an energy champion, unlocking the potential of individuals, teams, and organizations.

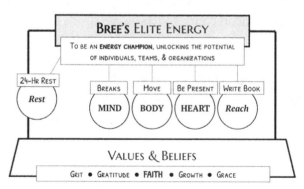

Image 17: Bree's Purpose Statement (source: Bree Bacon)

Energy represents capacity, my desired result. Advocating, speaking, facilitating, and coaching are the tools I use to unlock that capacity, and the people I strive to impact include individuals, teams, and organizations.

I want to help create a world where all three of these groups are able to unlock their full potential and achieve their unique purposes by cultivating their best capacity and overall well-being.

It is why I wrote this book. After burning out from neglecting my own well-being in the relentless pursuit of "productivity," I felt compelled to offer a different path—a framework designed to help individuals, teams, and organizations unlock their full potential.

YOUR *ELITE ENERGY* SYSTEM IS COMPLETE

Congratulations, your personal *Elite Energy* system is complete! If you are in a place where your purpose, your "why," feels clearly defined, go ahead and integrate it into your *Elite Energy* framework, available to print at www.BreeBacon.com.[7]

NEXT UP: PUTTING YOUR *ELITE ENERGY* SYSTEM INTO PRACTICE

You have established your foundational *Values & Beliefs*, committed to core wellness practices for your *Mind*, *Body*, and *Heart*, defined your approach to *Rest* and *Reach*, and even potentially added your overall "*why*."

Take a moment to celebrate your progress. Consider sharing your purpose statement with others by using the hashtag #YourEliteEnergy_Purpose. You can also share your full ecosystem by posting your completed *Elite Energy* framework with the hashtag #YourEliteEnergy.

Now that you have your framework, in part III, we will discuss how to put your system into practice and turn your commitments into action.

PART III

PUTTING YOUR SYSTEM INTO PRACTICE

CHAPTER 10

RHYTHM, BALANCE, AND SEASONS

———

"It doesn't matter if you work harder or smarter; if you neglect to also nurture a steady personal pulse, your success will be short-lived."

—Dr. Jacinta M. Jiménez

A fun science fact for you: In an ideal world, Newton's pendulum would swing forever, its motion a perfect back-and-forth that never loses momentum.[1]

In reality, when you release the first ball, it begins with strong, sharp clicks. Over time, however, the motion gradually slows and eventually stops. Why? Because *friction* is always at work.[2] It is the invisible force that slowly drains the energy, bringing motion to a halt.

The same is true in our lives. No matter how ideal our intentions, friction is inevitable. We do not live in a perfect world or a perfectly controlled environment. Some mornings, I hit the snooze button and miss my *Body* commitment to move. Other days, the stress piles up, and I struggle with my *Heart* commitment to be fully present with my loved ones. At times I *Reach* too much, I do not *Rest* enough, or I fail to align my actions with my foundational *Values & Beliefs*.

And you know what? That is okay.

This is where the *Elite Energy* framework steps in. It is a system, visual structure, and a language that helps you check in with yourself and communicate your needs, whether to yourself or to others. When you are not feeling at your best, it is an opportunity to pause and reflect:

- Am I staying true to my foundational *Values & Beliefs*?
- Am I investing enough in my *Mind*, *Body*, and *Heart*?
- Do I need more *Rest*, or am I over-resting and ready to *Reach*?
- Am I connected to the *"why"* behind everything I am doing for my *Elite Energy* system, my purpose?

Now that you have defined your number one commitment for each component of your *Elite Energy* system, it is time to put your commitments into practice.

In this chapter, we will focus on practical application as we explore how to transform these elements into a rhythm that aligns with your life. You will reflect on the balance of your components and learn how to evolve your *Elite Energy* system to adapt to the changes life brings, ensuring the framework helps you bring your best self forward, no matter what season you are navigating.

FINDING YOUR RHYTHM

In the context of your *Elite Energy* system, imagine pulling your *Rest* ball away from the others and releasing it. As it swings, it strikes the *core* balls, *Mind, Body,* and *Heart,* transferring its energy. The force travels through the core, pushing the *Reach* ball into the air. That ball swings back, creating a rhythm as it strikes the core balls again—*click, click, click*, a steady, back-and-forth rhythm.

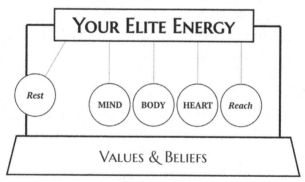

Image 18: Your Elite Energy Framework (source: Bree Bacon)

Humans are naturally drawn to rhythm. It underpins the way we speak, the way we move, and the way we think. Rhythm plays a fundamental role in our lives, from biological rhythms that regulate sleep-wake cycles, hormone secretion, and metabolism, to social rhythms that govern our interactions.[3] Even cognitive functions like memory, attention, and learning are enhanced by the rhythmic patterns of music.[4]

The same applies to your *Elite Energy* system. Just as rhythm governs our lives, your system requires rhythm to function at its best. Consider two types of rhythm you can apply to your *Elite Energy* system: steady and varied.

STEADY RHYTHMS

Steady rhythms are the wellness practices you commit to regularly (daily, weekly, or otherwise) that support each component of your system. These habits nourish your *Values & Beliefs*, your core (*Mind, Body, Heart*), and your practices of *Rest* and *Reach*. Over time, they accumulate to support your overall well-being, helping you operate at your personal best capacity.

As Brad Stulberg, author of *Peak Performance*, shares: "The best performers are not consistently great, they are great at being consistent."[5]

This is the key to unlocking your *Elite Energy*. For your commitments to truly lead to your best capacity, they need to be practiced regularly. Consistency is not just a nice-to-have; it is essential. Without regularly committing to the practices that fuel your *Mind, Body, Heart, Rest*, and *Reach*, you will not see the lasting benefits.

Like planting seeds but never watering them, you might see a few sprouts initially, but without consistent care, they will not grow into a thriving garden. Only through repeated, intentional action will your *Elite Energy* begin to compound, allowing you to operate at your fullest potential and sustain it over time.

Having a regular rhythm to your system does not just support your well-being; it also reduces stress and anxiety, giving you a sense of control. Research supports this: A study from Tel Aviv University found that predictable, repetitive routines can help lower anxiety and promote calm.[6] Northwestern Medicine adds that routines can help manage stress more effectively, improve sleep, encourage healthier eating, and increase physical activity.[7]

How do we turn your *Elite Energy* commitments into a steady rhythm? We will map them into a regular routine. Before we pursue this exercise in the "Reflect, Process, Apply" section toward the end of this chapter, consider this: Have you ever felt stuck, as if your pendulum had stopped swinging and lost its energy?

If so, you might feel either unchallenged and bored or overwhelmed with no clear path to relief. In either case, the solution could lie in adjusting your rhythm.

VARIED RHYTHMS

While steady rhythms provide the foundation for consistency and stability, varied rhythms can offer a necessary change, refreshing your system or giving it a burst of joy or rest. Just as you need the contrast of *Rest* and *Reach*, sometimes a variation in rhythm helps break the monotony and re-energizes your overall flow.

For example, let's discuss your *Body*. Research shows that variation in exercise routines is one of the best ways to maintain engagement. Christopher Janelle, an assistant professor at the University of Florida, states, "It gets monotonous if you're doing the same thing over and over. If you vary the routine, there's a significant increase in enjoyment that leads to greater adherence."[8]

Variation can also stimulate creativity and new ways of thinking. A change in your steady rhythm might open new possibilities or offer fresh perspectives on familiar problems. It could help you grow, learn, and discover new ways to better achieve or even find your purpose.

If you want to challenge your *Mind*, a variation in your steady rhythm might involve attending an annual retreat or signing up for an online course. On the other hand, if you are feeling overstimulated and overwhelmed, a variation could be taking a day (or even a week) without commitments, giving your *Mind* a break.

If you are not feeling challenged in your *Heart*, your relational health and wellness, you could switch things up by planning a weekend getaway with loved ones, joining a new social group, or volunteering for a cause you care about. Alternatively, if you are feeling over-stimulated, a change might mean dedicating more time to self-care, like scheduling regular date nights, taking a solo retreat, or enjoying a quiet night to yourself to recharge and reset.

The key is finding the rhythm that works for you and creates your best energy.

In the "Reflect, Process, Apply" section, I will guide you to reflect on which of your commitments should be part of a steady rhythm (whether daily or weekly) and where you might benefit from adding some variation (perhaps monthly or annually). Ultimately, it is about finding the rhythm that works best for your *Elite Energy* system, one that helps you maintain balance, manage stress, and unlock your best capacity in each season of life.

LET'S TALK ABOUT BALANCE...

This might not be news to you, but for Newton's pendulum to work effectively, all the balls need a solid foundation and must be the same size and weight. The device relies on the transfer of momentum from one ball to the next during collisions. If the balls were different in size or weight, the momentum transfer would be disrupted, leading to unpredictable behavior and a loss of energy.[9]

The same principle applies to your *Elite Energy* system. For your system to function optimally, balance is essential. Imbalance between the components can lead to unpredictable outcomes and, eventually, burnout—the very opposite of *Elite Energy*.

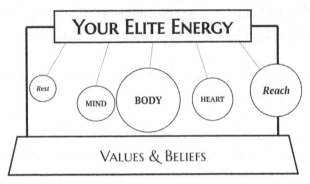

Image 19: Balance (source: Bree Bacon)

Let's say you are laser-focused on your physical health. You work out every day, eat super healthy, and prioritize sleep. However, if you neglect your *Heart* (relational health) or your *Mind* (mental health), your overall energy and well-being will suffer. Similarly, if you are constantly in *Reach* mode, taking on challenge after challenge without giving yourself time to properly *Rest* and recharge, you will quickly deplete your energy reserves.

I know this all too well. For my own *Elite Energy* system, I had to face the truth that I tend to *Reach* too much. I love the thrill of learning new skills, setting new goals, and pushing myself to achieve. The sense of accomplishment that comes from overcoming challenges is motivating, but there is a catch: Constantly challenging myself without adequate *Rest* and reflection can hold me back from truly reaching my best capacity. In fact, pushing too hard can lead to burnout and exhaustion, leaving me far from my *Elite Energy*.

Are your components balanced? Are you giving equal attention to your foundation, your *Mind, Body, Heart*, how you *Rest* and *Reach*?

It is easy to get caught up in one area while neglecting the others, but true *Elite Energy* comes from harmony between all aspects of your system. We will reflect more on this shortly in our application section, where you will assess how well your components are aligned and adjust to ensure your system is balanced.

SEASONS: RECALIBRATING YOUR SYSTEM

During the research phase for this book, I had the pleasure of meeting Kara Hardin, a registered psychotherapist and the lead executive officer and founder of The Practice Lab. Kara holds a doctor of law (JD) from the University of Toronto and a master's in psychology and counseling from the University of St. Thomas. Her organization provides mental health training to high-achieving individuals, teams, and organizations.

I shared my *Elite Energy* framework with Kara and sought her insights. She appreciated the clarity and visual representation of how different aspects of ourselves are interconnected: *Mind, Body,* and *Heart*. However, one point she raised struck me deeply: the importance of adapting our *Elite Energy* system as we move through different phases or seasons of life.

As she put it, "What someone does for their *Elite Energy* in their early twenties will differ from what they might require after having a child. We need to grant ourselves grace and acceptance, recognizing that our methods for nurturing our *Elite Energy* can evolve as we move through different stages of life."

Kara is absolutely right about seasons. Just as nature goes through distinct seasons, each with its own rhythm of growth, rest, and renewal, our lives also follow different phases, each requiring us to adapt how we approach our *Elite Energy* commitments. We each have seasons when we are driven to push forward, taking on new challenges, growing our careers, or building relationships. At other times we have seasons when we need to slow down, reflect, and prioritize rest.

Life moves through times of intense activity and moments of stillness, with each season calling for different investments in your *Elite Energy* system. Your system must shift accordingly. What works for you in one season may no longer serve you in another. The key is learning how to adapt our commitments, whether it is focusing on self-care and recovery during quieter seasons or ramping up our efforts when we are ready to stretch and grow.

Reflecting on my own experience, I can see that I went through a season of deep mourning after the loss of six pregnancies, mixed with the overwhelming anxiety that came with the birth of my miracle daughter, Eliana. Instead of stepping back during that season, granting myself grace to mourn and heal, or allowing for rest and reflection, I pushed forward. I overinflated my *Reach*, adding more and more responsibilities to fill the space, thinking it was the path to healing, to feeling like myself again.

The result was predictable. My *Elite Energy* system went into overdrive and ultimately collapsed. What I learned, though, is that sometimes a major crash and burn is not a failure. It is a reset.

What season are you in right now? Are you in a season of career growth, ready to take on a bigger challenge or step into a leadership role? Or perhaps you are in a season focused on family, where your energy is devoted to creating strong, meaningful connections at home. Maybe you are in a season of giving back, looking to increase your involvement with your community or devoting more time to volunteering. Whatever season you find yourself in, recognize that each one has its own rhythm and needs, and the key is to align your *Elite Energy* system with your needs in that season to bring out the best in you.

REFLECT, PROCESS, APPLY

Your turn: This is where we take your commitments and translate them into actionable routines, ensuring your system is balanced and reasonable for your current life season. Take a moment to revisit your top commitments for each aspect of your *Elite Energy* system (refer to your completed worksheet from part II).

STEP ONE: MAP OUT YOUR STEADY RHYTHM

Begin by plotting how you will integrate your commitments into a regular routine, whether that is daily, weekly, or otherwise. Below is a simple rhythm grid to help you get organized. Start by outlining your primary commitments for each component of your *Elite Energy* system and consider whether they are daily, weekly, or monthly practices. You may also want to include additional wellness goals you are considering integrating into your regular routine.

Elite Energy	Daily	Weekly	Monthly	Yearly
Values & Beliefs				
Mind				
Body				
Heart				
Rest				
Reach				

Table #1: Your Elite Energy Rhythm (Source: Bree Bacon)

STEP TWO: LAYER IN YOUR VARIED RHYTHM

Next, take a few minutes to think about how you can introduce strategic variation into your *Elite Energy* routine. While steady rhythms offer consistency, varied rhythms are essential for rejuvenating your energy and infusing your routine with excitement, joy, or necessary *Rest*. Variations can break the monotony and spark a sense of renewal.

For example, a yearly race can energize your *Body*. Committing to a mindfulness retreat with a partner once a year can deepen your connection to your *Heart* and *Mind* (two for one!). Reflect on your rhythm grid from above and layer in some intentional variation.

STEP THREE: ARE YOU BALANCED?

Take a step back and assess your chart. Are the different elements of your *Elite Energy* system balanced? Look closely at your grid and ask yourself:

- Are you nurturing each aspect of yourself equally?
- Do your *Rest* commitments match your need for recovery? Do you have a need for an additional *Reach* goal?
- Do you have any commitments that you may need to remove or adjust to recalibrate your balance?

This is your opportunity to ensure you are investing in your whole self, not over-prioritizing one area at the expense of another. Edit your chart as needed.

STEP FOUR: YOUR CURRENT SEASON

Take a moment to reflect on the season of life you are in right now. Life's different stages, whether joyful, challenging, or somewhere in between, require us to adjust the way we allocate our energy.

Begin by thinking about how each component of your *Elite Energy* system has evolved over time.

- How have your *Values & Beliefs* shifted?
- In what ways have your *Mind*, *Body*, and *Heart* priorities changed?
- How has your approach to *Rest* and *Reach* adjusted over the years?

Once you have reflected on these shifts, consider how your current season might call for adjustments. Are you in a major transition, like welcoming a child, starting a new job, or experiencing a loss? In these moments, some components of your *Elite Energy* system may need more attention than others. For example, do you need to prioritize *Rest* in this phase, or recalibrate your goals for *Reach*? Do your *Mind, Body,* or *Heart* commitments need to evolve to better align with your current realities?

Revisit your *Elite Energy* chart and adjust it as needed. This could mean scaling back certain commitments, introducing new ones, or rebalancing the way you allocate energy to different areas. The goal is to ensure your *Elite Energy* system aligns with your present season, so you can optimize your energy and maintain balance while navigating life's changes.

AN EXAMPLE: BREE'S *ELITE ENERGY*

When I worked through these exercises myself, I began by revisiting my commitments from part II. Below is a refresher:

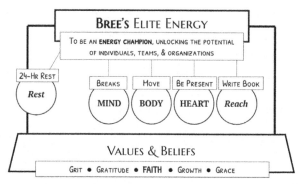

Image 20: Bree's Elite Energy Worksheet (source: Bree Bacon)

Next, I mapped them out into my steady rhythm, adding in a few extra commitments I was considering as well.

Elite Energy	Daily	Weekly	Monthly	Yearly
Values & Beliefs	Morning reflection	Church service		
Mind	Three twenty-minute breaks			
Body	Thirty-minute workout	Rest day		
Heart	Dinner together	Volunteer		
Rest		Sunday Rest		
Reach	Thirty-minute writing			

Table #2: Bree's Steady Rhythm (Source: Bree Bacon)

I then added some variations to the routine: a monthly massage, an annual retreat, and potentially signing up for a psychology course.

Elite Energy	Daily	Weekly	Monthly	Yearly
Values & Beliefs	Morning reflection	Church service		Annual retreat
Mind	Three twenty-minute breaks	Psychology course		
Body	Thirty-minute workout	Rest day	Massage	
Heart	Dinner together	Volunteer		
Rest		Sunday Rest		
Reach	Thirty-minute writing			Release my book!

Table #3: Bree's Varied Rhythm (Source: Bree Bacon)

Finally, I reviewed my balance and considered my current season. In this phase of my life, I felt I needed to prioritize *Rest* more, so I added extra self-care practices like "Evening chill time" and "Stay-at-home weeks," while reducing some activities. For example, I decided right now is probably not the best time to add a psychology course to my load, so I crossed that out.

Elite Energy	Daily	Weekly	Monthly	Yearly
Values & Beliefs	Morning reflection	Church service		~~Annual retreat~~
Mind	Three twenty-minute breaks	~~Psychology course~~		
Body	Thirty-minute workout	Rest day	(Quarterly) Massage	
Heart	Dinner together	Volunteer		
Rest	Evening chill time	Sunday Rest		Stay at home week
Reach	Thirty-minute writing			Release my book!

Table #4: Bree's Rhythm Grid (Source: Bree Bacon)

Rhythm, balance, and seasons are key elements to keep in mind as you apply your *Elite Energy* system. By establishing a steady rhythm, incorporating intentional variations, and maintaining balance across the different components of your system, you will create a sustainable path to your best capacity and overall well-being.

Your *Elite Energy* system is not a rigid set of rules but a framework to help you live intentionally and take care of yourself as you move through different seasons of life. The framework is meant to evolve with you, empowering you to embrace each season of life with clarity and confidence on what is going to bring your personal best capacity and overall well-being.

Of course, not all seasons are easy. Some can be downright tough. In the next chapter, we will explore how to activate your *Elite Energy* system when life gets challenging, ensuring you can stay grounded even when times are hard.

CHAPTER 11

WHEN LIFE GETS HARD

———

"Everything can be taken from a man but one thing: the last of the human freedoms—to choose one's attitude in any given set of circumstances, to choose one's own way."

—VIKTOR FRANKL

Up to 90 percent of people will experience at least one traumatic event in their lifetime.[1]

What is trauma? The American Psychological Association defines it as an emotional response to a distressing event, whether that event is an accident, crime, natural disaster, abuse, violence, the death of a loved one, or war.[2] Mental Health America further clarifies that trauma is "an emotional response to distressing event or situation that breaks your sense of security."[3] This event could be a singular moment or a series of deeply upsetting experiences perceived as life-threatening or profoundly damaging.

What is critical to remember is that trauma is uniquely personal. People process experiences in vastly different ways, and not everyone reacts to the same event in the same manner. What one person may perceive as traumatic might not have the same impact on another.[4]

I want to take a moment to acknowledge that trauma is an incredibly vast and deeply personal topic, one that goes far beyond the scope of this book or my own expertise. I do not claim to fully understand the unique challenges of your lived experiences, but what I *can* offer is a glimpse into my own journey.

Like many, I have faced some difficult and challenging moments in my life. I would like to share how I used the *Elite Energy* framework during and after that time. This framework not only help me regain my best capacity, it helped me function, heal, and restore a sense of balance and well-being. In the chapter ahead, I will share the story of how this framework supported me through my own stormy season and how it may help you navigate yours.

MY STORMY SEASON

When I reflect on my journey, I realize that trauma was not just a single event. It was a prolonged season of loss, uncertainty, and emotional turmoil. It was a time when life seemed to challenge me at every turn.

First, as you already know, while my husband and I tried to start a family, we faced the heartache of recurrent pregnancy loss. We lost five babies before we were finally blessed with our daughter, Eliana, and then we lost another child during pregnancy after her. The emotional and physical toll of these losses is something I still carry with me. Seeing my babies' heartbeats on the ultrasound, feeling a sense of hope, only to then face the crushing reality that those heartbeats had stopped—each loss left a lasting scar.

My second deeply challenging experience was the birth of my miracle baby, Eliana. While the birth itself was a joyous occasion, it quickly became complicated, requiring several hours of surgery for me afterward. Just when I thought the worst was behind me, I was rushed to the emergency room with postpartum preeclampsia. This series of events set off an overwhelming wave of postpartum anxiety that lingered throughout Eliana's first year. I was consumed by fear. Not only for my own health and survival but, even more so, for the well-being and safety of my miracle child.

My third traumatic experience, which I will describe below, occurred at a time when I thought I had finally found my footing. By the summer of 2022, I had developed the *Elite Energy* framework and had begun to envision bringing it to life for others. Before I could fully step into that vision, life threw me another curveball—a traumatic experience that challenged me to apply the framework, all while navigating a new reality.

STORM NUMBER THREE
In the fall of 2022, after stepping down from my leadership role to prioritize my health, I thought I had successfully

reset my life. I had made changes to reduce stress and create a more balanced routine. I started a new job at a smaller company, working with an executive I had previously worked with and admired. My miracle baby girl, Eliana, had just turned one, so the constant anxiety around things like sudden infant death syndrome (SIDS) and other early childhood fears began to ease. I felt like I was in a better place.

After completely burning out earlier that previous summer, I was determined to live with more balance. I committed myself to practicing the *Elite Energy* principles I had created for myself. Every morning, I woke up early for some quiet time, reflecting on my *Values & Beliefs*. I made time for a quick workout, fueling my *Body*, before Eliana woke up. At work, I challenged my *Mind* by learning a new business model and team dynamics, while also being mindful to take mental breaks throughout the day to recharge. Most importantly, I made my relationships a priority, my *Heart*, spending quality time with Eliana and my husband and saying no to late-night meetings that could steal precious moments from them.

Despite my earnest efforts, I found myself sinking into the darkest depression I had ever experienced. Each morning, the simple act of getting out of bed felt like an insurmountable task. It was sheer determination, driven by my sense of duty to my daughter and my job, that got me up each day. Night after night, I would cry myself to sleep, dreading the thought of facing another day. Guilt weighed heavily on me: *Had my husband and I brought a daughter into this world just so she could feel the way I was feeling?*

Before this chapter in my life, I had never truly understood depression. Now, I was living in the depths of it. Neither my husband nor I knew how to pull me out of the nightmare.

I sought out doctors, but the ones I could get in to see quickly just glanced at me and said, "What drug do you want to be on?" That response baffled me. I assumed that before jumping into medication, we should first understand *why* I felt this way and what needed to change. How was I supposed to know what medication to take? What were the side effects? Was it worth it? Would it mask an underlying issue? Would it make things worse?

I reached out to my OBGYN, but she explained that she was legally unable to offer me the help I needed, handing me a postcard with an email address that promised a twenty-four-hour response time. I emailed twice. No reply.

I turned to my church, meeting with two compassionate pastors who tried to connect me with a Christian psychologist. I also reached out to her twice. No reply.

We sought emergency resources my husband had access to through the military. However, the therapist we were assigned seemed overwhelmed by the depth of my distress and unable to help.

I felt incredibly alone. I had always been someone who was driven, determined, and focused on finding solutions. Yet, for the first time in my life, I was the one desperately in need of help. I needed any kind of insight or guidance to pull me out of the hole I was in. No matter where I turned, doors kept slamming in my face.

Finally, after several months of this constant struggle, one night while my husband put our daughter to sleep, I found myself alone and consumed by misery in our bathroom. I had reached the bottom of the barrel. I had no more human avenues to turn to for help. I had exhausted all my options and still found no answers.

If you remember from chapter 4, the foundation of my *Elite Energy* system, my values and beliefs, is my faith—a belief in Jesus and the Bible. In that moment of utter desperation, I turned to my faith. Staring at my reflection in the bathroom mirror, I cried out, "God, what is wrong with me?"

In the silence, I actually heard an answer.

"Do a breast check."

In case anyone is curious, before this moment I had never personally focused on doing breast checks. My primary care physician or OBGYN conducted them during my annual visits. I had no history of breast cancer in my family, so it was never something that was top of mind. I was also thirty-eight years old at the time, too young to even qualify for a mammogram. I had physicals and assessments over the previous year, especially after having my baby, and no one had found anything unusual.

In that moment, as I stood there, crying and staring at myself in the bathroom mirror, I listened. I did a breast check. I found a lump.

What followed was a whirlwind of appointments, tests, and scans that revealed not just one but four lumps—two tumors in my right breast and two more in my lymph nodes under my arm.

I had stage three, triple negative breast cancer.

I was referred to an oncologist and met with him in December of 2022 to fully understand what my diagnosis meant. When he walked into the room, he told my husband and me that I had an aggressive form of breast cancer, and at that moment my chance of survival was about 50 percent. To fight it, I would need to start six months of chemotherapy immediately. After that, I would undergo surgery to remove the tumors and lymph nodes, followed by several weeks of daily radiation and another several months of immunotherapy infusions. The entire treatment plan would take about a year to complete.

I went into shock. *I have a one-year-old daughter, how could this be happening? What do you mean I have a 50 percent chance of survival? Six months of chemotherapy? Where is the simple ten-day pill that you take for normal illnesses? How did this happen? No one in my family has ever had breast cancer. I don't have any of the genetic markers for it. Where did this come from?*

In that moment, I went numb. My *Elite Energy* system was experiencing a major earthquake, and everything I had worked to put into balance was now in total chaos.

At that moment, I could not think about my mental, physical, or emotional health; about maintaining rhythm; or even about balancing *Rest* and *Reach*. All I could do was hold tight to my foundation.

DURING THE STORM, HOLD TIGHT TO YOUR FOUNDATION

During the six months of chemotherapy and surgery, that is all I did—hold tight to my foundation, my *Values & Beliefs*, as I survived one day at a time.

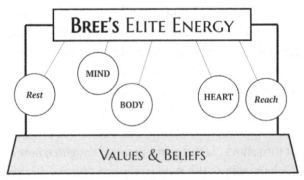

Image 21: During the Storm, Hold Tight to Your Foundation (source: Bree Bacon)

During my storm of cancer, my usual rhythms—*Mind, Body, Heart, Rest,* and *Reach*—were gone. I even went numb when it came to praying. What I did witness was my husband, family, friends, and an entire community surrounding me with prayer and support. I watched as God provided a team of oncologists, doctors, surgeons, and nurses who carried me through. I just survived, observing it all unfold. It was humbling, especially for a control freak like me, a traditionally "Miss Independent" woman (thank you, Kelly Clarkson).

What you have defined as the foundation of your *Elite Energy* system is what helps you navigate difficult situations. It provides clarity and stability when everything else feels uncertain. Your foundation defines who you are, what you stand for, and gives you a sense of direction, even in chaos.

I believe the storms of life can either challenge or solidify our foundation, testing what we believe and offering new insights. In my case, cancer brought my faith in God to a whole new level. Before this, I had always approached my faith intellectually. I studied the Bible, attended church, volunteered, donated, and strived for perfection. Though I knew, at an intellectual level, that I could not "earn" acceptance, I was still somehow always caught in the cycle of trying.

The night I heard, "Do a breast check," staring into my bathroom mirror, marked the first time I audibly heard God's answer to one of my prayers so clearly. It took me back to the story of Elijah in 1 Kings: "A great and powerful wind tore the mountains apart and shattered the rocks before the Lord, but the Lord was not in the wind. After the wind there was an earthquake, but the Lord was not in the earthquake. After the earthquake came a fire, but the Lord was not in the fire. And after the fire came a gentle whisper."[5]

God's voice was not in the wind, the earthquake, or the fire. In my case, all the noise of the world had to be silenced. The doors were slammed shut by doctors, pastors, therapists, experts, and even my own attempts to control things until I could finally hear that gentle whisper. I will forever be in awe of that moment when my prayer was answered so clearly.

As I reflect on surviving that storm, holding tight to my foundation is what carried me through, and it is something I would encourage anyone facing their own storm to consider.

Equally important is giving yourself grace. If you are in the middle of a storm or have just emerged from one, do not put pressure on yourself for your *Elite Energy* system to be running at full capacity. Give yourself time, grace, and patience.

When you are ready, hit the reset button.

HITTING "RESET"

Back to my story. Amazingly, at surgery, I experienced another miracle: The cancer was all dead. It bumped my survival curve from 50 percent to over 90 percent. I still needed to undergo several weeks of daily radiation and then six additional months of immunotherapy infusions, but the news was incredible.

Even with this newfound hope, my *Elite Energy* system needed a serious reset. The earthquake had stopped, the balls were no longer flying in chaos, but now everything was still. My rhythm, the *click, click, click* of my *Elite Energy* system, needed a reboot.

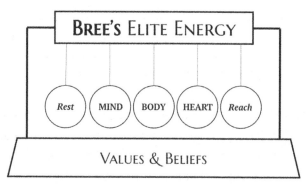

Image 22: Post Storm, A Still System (source: Bree Bacon)

To get my *Elite Energy* rhythm back in motion, back to truly living my life, something needed to pull back one of the end balls to restart the pendulum.

For those of us who tend to overachieve, it is tempting to jump back in by reaching for the next challenge or achievement. It is easy to distract ourselves by pushing harder, taking on more, and running after the next goal. I know the pull all too well, the desire to throw myself into "achieving" in order to feel like I am back on track. However, the National Alliance on Mental Illness (NAMI) emphasizes a crucial point: "After a major setback, we cannot afford to skip over taking care of ourselves."[6]

What we need most post-storm is to start with *Rest*.

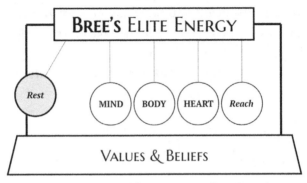

Image 23: Start with Rest (source: Bree Bacon)

Rest after a storm is a necessity for two key reasons. The first is to give yourself time to *recover*: physically, mentally, and emotionally. *Rest* is the essential space that allows you to heal from the toll of the chaos you have endured.

A quick science lesson from *Harvard Health*: When we experience stress, our brain triggers the "fight or flight" response, which starts in the amygdala. It sends a distress signal to the hypothalamus, which activates the autonomic nervous system to prepare the body to react quickly. This system has two parts: the sympathetic nervous system (like a gas pedal, speeding up heart rate and breathing for energy) and the parasympathetic nervous system (like a brake, helping the body relax once the danger is over). Chronic stress, however, can keep the body in this heightened state, leading to health problems like high blood pressure and anxiety. *Rest* is crucial because it helps activate the parasympathetic system, signaling to the body that the danger has passed and allowing the body to recover and reset.[7]

The Hospital for Special Surgery (HSS) in New York suggests several ways to support your parasympathetic nervous system and promote *Rest*, such as mild exercise, meditation, deep breathing, or nature walks.[8] The key is to find what works best for you to unwind and decompress. Whether it is enjoying long baths, getting a massage, reading, or listening to music, it is important to choose activities that relax and soothe you, not ones that add stress.

For me personally, I returned to my morning routine of starting the day with a cup of coffee, gratitude, and reflection. I also made sure to spend some extra quiet time by myself, taking long walks in nature and practicing deep breathing.

Bessel van der Kolk, author of *The Body Keeps The Score: Brain, Mind, and Body in The Healing of Trauma*, emphasizes that "the first order of business is to find ways to cope with feeling overwhelmed by the sensations and emotions associated with the past," but he also notes that "at the core of recovery is self-awareness."[9]

This is the second reason why *Rest* is essential. We need to give ourselves space and time to *process* the thoughts and emotions tied to our storm, reflecting on what happened and making sense of our experience. Van der Kolk advises, "Sooner or later you need to confront what has happened to you, but only after you feel safe and will not be retraumatized by it."[10]

I learned this personally. I had times I was not ready to talk about or even think about my difficult events because I was still too close to them. In those moments, I first focused on calming my nervous system, signaling to myself and my body I was safe and the storm had passed.

As I began to feel ready, processing everything that had happened became a crucial step in my recovery. I started the practice of reflection (emphasis on starting, as I still have moments I am not ready to revisit), not just about the cancer but also the miscarriages, postpartum preeclampsia, postpartum anxiety, depression, as well as my crash and burn experience.

Once I felt ready, I moved on to reigniting the *core* of my *Elite Energy* system: *Mind, Body, Heart.*

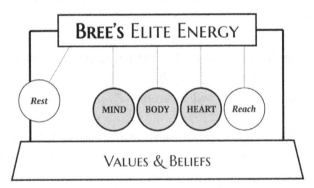

Image 24: Core: Mind, Body, & Heart (source: Bree Bacon)

Reinvesting in your *Mind, Body,* and *Heart* is key to regaining your energy and personal capacity. However, it is essential to approach this process with self-compassion. The *core* you had before the storm may need to shift as you adjust to your *Elite Energy* system's new normal. As you reenter life, it is important to set boundaries, prioritize your needs, and practice self-compassion in both your thoughts and actions.

For me, returning to my routine began with morning workouts, but I eased back in with yoga and long walks, not the intense workouts I used to do (my *Body*). I went back to work but made sure to take breaks and schedule time for mental rest throughout the day (my *Mind*). I also prioritized spending quality time with the most important people in my life, my daughter and husband (my *Heart*). I learned to say no to activities or meetings that would take time away from them, even signing up for a mommy-and-me dance class with my daughter Eliana after cancer had stolen so much of our time together.

Eventually, I reached a point where I was ready to challenge myself again. I was ready to *Reach*. I wanted to prove to myself I was still alive, still capable, and still able to pursue goals and dreams.

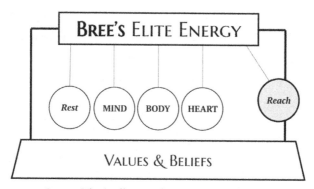

Image 25: Finally, Reach (source: Bree Bacon)

I believe that challenging yourself after tragedy can help shift your focus from dwelling on the past to looking forward to the future. By setting and achieving goals, you build momentum, which fosters optimism and resilience in the face of adversity. While taking on new challenges after such a difficult time may feel overwhelming, I think it can play a key role in healing. It can promote empowerment, growth, and a renewed sense of purpose and control.

For me, the first challenge I set after my cancer journey was a physical one: I decided to run my first-ever race, a half-marathon. I chose to do it around the one-year anniversary of my cancer surgery, a time when I had been in the worst condition of my life, having just survived six months of intensive chemotherapy and spent much of that time in bed.

My goal was not to push myself too hard or try to win. It was simply to complete the race and say, "Cancer, you don't get to win." I chose Grandma's Marathon in Duluth, Minnesota. The picture on the left was taken by my husband in June 2023, the day of my surgery. The picture on the right is from June 2024, one year later, as I ran my first ever half-marathon.

Image 26: June 2023 vs. June 2024 (source left:
Neil Bacon, source right: MarathonFoto)

My second *Reach* goal was writing this book, a mental (and maybe a little emotional) challenge for myself. My hope is that the *Elite Energy* system and my story will help at least one person who is struggling to find their footing.

What will my next goal be? I am not sure yet, and that is part of the fun of your *Elite Energy* system. Right? It is about taking moments to *Rest*, relax, enjoy life, and celebrate. Then, when you are ready, it is about defining and challenging yourself, doing things you have never done before and learning new skills; to live, grow, and discover.

That is how I rebounded and reset when life got hard and storms came my way. During the earthquake, I held tight to my foundational *Values & Beliefs*. After the earthquake, I began with *Rest,* taking a moment to acknowledge what I had just been through and process it. Then, I reestablished my *core*: the wellness habits that nurture and support my *Mind, Body,* and *Heart*. Finally, I set a *Reach* goal, diving back into life with my next challenge, all while carrying gratitude and a new perspective based on what I had just survived.

No official "Reflect, Process, Apply" section exists for this chapter. Instead, if you recently experienced a storm, ask yourself: *What is one small step I can take today to restore and prioritize my Elite Energy system during this time?*

If you are not currently in a storm, I hope this chapter equips you with the tools and perspective to help if life brings a challenge your way.

CONGRATS, YOUR LAST STEP!

Now that we have established your personal *Elite Energy* system, discussed how to create your rhythm, and explored how to rebuild when life gets hard, we are moving to our last step: creating a culture that encourages teams to prioritize their *Elite Energy* systems, making this a team sport.

CHAPTER 12

CREATING A CULTURE

---

*"Teamwork begins by building trust. And
the only way to do that is to overcome
our need for invulnerability."*

—PATRICK LENCIONI

Have you ever considered the true power of a team's collective energy? It is not just about the hours worked or tasks completed. What could be accomplished if every team member operated at their best capacity?

This is where the magic of creating a culture around your *Elite Energy* comes into play.

Imagine a workplace where every individual feels comfortable sharing their wellness needs and is supported in pursuing their best capacity. A place where well-being is not an afterthought but a core pillar; where every individual is empowered to thrive *Mind*, *Body*, and *Heart*. Here, people are encouraged to balance the need for *Rest* with the drive to *Reach*, to share their purpose, and stay grounded in their personal *Values & Beliefs*. It is a culture where wellness is not just a personal pursuit but a shared commitment that fuels the entire team's collective potential.

Building a culture around *Elite Energy* does more than just improve individual performance; it creates a dynamic environment where the collective energy of the team drives greater success. This chapter is about transforming the personal *Elite Energy* system you have built into a shared experience. From fostering accountability to enhancing deeper connections, the benefits of creating this culture are profound.

Let's explore why making *Elite Energy* a team sport is not just a smart move, it is vital to your success and the success of your team or organization.

RATIONALE #1: ACCOUNTABILITY FOR YOU

Did you know that simply sharing a commitment or goal can increase your chances of success by 65 percent?[1] In fact, when you have regular check-ins with a partner, your likelihood of success jumps to 95 percent.[2]

The first reason to make *Elite Energy* a team sport is for your personal success. When you share your commitments with others, you are not just accountable to yourself, you are also accountable to your partner or team. The support, encouragement, and fresh perspectives that come from having someone alongside you can make all the difference. Regular check-ins provide ongoing motivation, help you navigate challenges, and introduce new strategies and approaches for incorporating your *Elite Energy* system into everyday life.

Sharing your wellness commitments with others can give you a real boost. For example, if one of your goals is to walk every day, you could share your commitment using #YourEliteEnergy_Body and post daily pictures of your walk. Or, invite a friend or coworker to join you. If you are remote, schedule the time on your calendars and catch up with your friend or coworker while on the phone and both walking. Even better, make it a team activity. Host "Wednesday Walks," where different pairs of colleagues team up for virtual walking breaks. It is a win for both physical health and social connection.

No matter what wellness habits you commit to, whether it is exercise, eating healthy, mindfulness, or something else, doing them with a partner or group will amplify your commitment, motivation, and enjoyment. By turning your *Elite Energy* into a shared experience, you not only increase the chances of sticking with your habits long-term, but you also foster a more supportive, engaged, and energized environment for yourself, your team, and your organization.

RATIONALE #2: CAPACITY AND WELL-BEING OF YOUR TEAM

The second reason to turn your *Elite Energy* into a team sport is to enhance your team's capacity and well-being. If investing in your own *Elite Energy* system leads to a more energized, productive, and fulfilled version of you, imagine the impact on your team when everyone operates at their best.

Remember the three case studies from chapter 3:

- **Wachovia Bank**: 106 employees participated in an energy management program, focusing on physical, emotional, and mental wellness. After three months, they saw a 13 percentage point increase in loan revenue, outperforming the control group.[3]

- **Kent State University (KSU)**: KSU enhanced their Employee Assistance Program (EAP), providing support for stress, anxiety, and other issues. This led to a reduction in depression-related claims, saving almost $5,000 per employee annually, totaling over $1 million in one year.[4]

- **9-1-1 dispatchers**: 40 percent of LAPD dispatchers reported burnout. Over six weeks, five hundred dispatchers received weekly emails sharing colleagues' stories, fostering community and support. The intervention was modeled to reduced burnout and turnover by 50 percent, leading to significant cost savings.[5]

Each case study illustrates how prioritizing employee well-being boosts capacity, increases productivity, reduces health care costs, and decreases turnover, all of which positively impact an organization's overall health and performance.

By making *Elite Energy* the foundation of your team or organization's culture, you get the double-whammy: a team that prioritizes individual well-being and is better equipped to perform at their best capacity for your organization and its mission. A well-supported team is a high-performing team, and that directly translates to stronger individuals, more energized teams, and a healthier organization.

RATIONALE #3: TEAM BUILDING

The average person will spend ninety thousand hours at work.[6] That is about a third of your life! Given our innate need for social connection, it is no surprise that nearly 70 percent of employees say they would be happier with deeper relationships with their colleagues, and more than two-thirds express a desire to move beyond surface-level interactions at work.[7]

People want to feel seen and known for more than just their job skills. They crave a deeper sense of belonging and recognition. When colleagues, teammates, and managers acknowledge individuals as whole people, understanding their personal values, interests, and unique needs, it fosters a stronger connection in the workplace.

When people are known and well-connected, it benefits both them and your organization. Teams that are highly connected experience a 21 percent boost in profitability compared to their less-connected peers.[8] Teams in the top 20 percent for connectedness also see 41 percent less absenteeism and 59 percent lower employee turnover.[9]

A deeper sense of being seen and understood fosters trust and camaraderie, creating a more supportive and engaging workplace. Employees feel valued not only for their contributions but for who they are as individuals, enriching their overall experience and enhancing their sense of fulfillment at work.

Establishing and sharing *Elite Energy* systems within your team is a powerful way to build deeper connections. It allows everyone to move beyond skill sets and gain insight into what fuels each other's best capacity. What *Values & Beliefs* are foundational for each individual? What commitments does each teammate have in *Mind*, *Body*, and *Heart*? How do they prefer to *Rest* or recharge, and what are their stretch or *Reach* goals? Where do the team's systems align and where are the differences?

Leveraging the *Elite Energy* framework as a team activity offers a valuable opportunity to step away from the day-to-day grind and engage in meaningful conversations. It gives team members a chance to reveal who they are beyond the typical video calls or spreadsheets. By understanding what is important to each person, the team builds a better understanding and empathy for each other, opening the door to supporting one another's personal best capacity and well-being.

REFLECT, PROCESS, APPLY
Your turn: You can transform your *Elite Energy* into a team-focused activity in various ways, boosting team building, leadership development, and overall

organizational culture. Visit www.BreeBacon.com to explore different options, including sessions led by me, designed to help you implement these practices within your team or organization.[10]

INTRODUCE ELITE ENERGY

Start by introducing the concept of *Elite Energy* to your team. Here are several approaches you can take to introduce this framework to your team or organization:

- **Book club**: Organize a structured book club where team members read specific sections of the *Elite Energy* material, then gather periodically to discuss key insights, themes, and how they have defined their own *Elite Energy* systems.

- **Facilitated team workshop**: Book a facilitated workshop where your team is guided through the process of defining their personal *Elite Energy* systems. This interactive experience will help your team complete their personal frameworks while also providing opportunities to learn from each other's approaches and insights, strengthening team connections.

- **Event keynote**: I offer talks tailored to teams, companies, or industry events where I introduce the principles of *Elite Energy* and share practical insights on improving energy, capacity, and well-being.

By having your leaders and employees participate in one of the options above, you demonstrate that prioritizing well-being is a core value within your team, ultimately fostering a more engaged, high-capacity workforce ready to contribute to the organization's mission.

REGULAR CHECK-INS

Whatever method you choose for introducing *Elite Energy* to your team or organization, regular check-ins are key to ensuring everyone is putting their system into practice. Here are some ideas to help keep the momentum going:

- **Daily or weekly reflection**: Set up a regular calendar hold where team members either start their day or week reflecting on how they will invest in their *Elite Energy* and re-commitment to their wellness practices.

- **Regular team huddles**: Organize team huddles to check in on commitments; share updates, successes, and challenges; and remind everyone of the organization's commitment to their personal *Elite Energy* systems and overall well-being. I recommend holding these monthly and making them more casual, like a lunch session, to foster open, relaxed conversation and encourage authentic sharing.

- **A physical, visual reminder**: *Elite Energy* pendulums are available for purchase at www.BreeBacon.com.[11] I keep one on my desk as a visual reminder throughout my day to check in on my *Elite Energy* system and how I am nurturing my ecosystem to support my best capacity and overall well-being.

LEADERSHIP SHADOW

As a leader, demonstrating a healthy *Elite Energy* system is important not only for your own well-being but also for the well-being of your team. Your team observes your example closely, and they will see if you sacrifice your mental, emotional, and physical health for the job. Burn the midnight oil, and they will likely feel pressured to do the same.

This is sometimes referred to as your "leadership shadow," the unconscious influence a leader has on their team. By committing to, demonstrating, and openly sharing how you prioritize your own *Elite Energy* system, you encourage your team to do the same. This helps everyone maintain their best capacity and fosters a healthier and more sustainable work culture.

FINAL EXERCISE

As a final exercise, take a moment to reflect on how you will contribute to creating a culture around *Elite Energy* within your team or organization. Whether it is finding an accountability partner, facilitating this exercise for your team, or organizing regular team huddles to discuss well-being, choose one action you can take to create a lasting impact.

I commit to: _____

YOU DID IT!

You have fully embraced your *Elite Energy* system, learning how to create a rhythm, find balance, and adapt to the various seasons of life. You have seen how I personally leveraged this framework during my recovery from cancer, and I hope that serves as inspiration for you when life throws challenges your way. Now you are ready to transform your personal *Elite Energy* system into a team-driven culture that fosters lasting success and well-being. By sharing your system and engaging others, you foster accountability, spark motivation, and create a supportive environment that unlocks everyone's best capacity.

When teams prioritize well-being, the impact is clear: improved capacity, deeper engagement, and stronger connections. As a leader, your commitment to *Elite Energy* serves as a powerful example for your team. Whether through regular check-ins or sharing personal wellness goals, small actions create a ripple effect that cultivates a culture of health, wellness, and well-being, driving both individual and organizational success.

I hope you are inspired to take what you have learned and lay the foundation for a culture of sustainable success, one that not only unlocks your best capacity but inspires those around you to grow and thrive alongside you.

CLOSING REFLECTIONS

———

"Act as if what you do makes a difference. It does."
—WILLIAM JAMES

Throughout our time together, I hope it has become abundantly clear that defining, nurturing, and investing in your *Elite Energy* system is not just a choice; it is a vital necessity. It is essential for combating the burnout that has become so pervasive in our culture, unlocking your best capacity and creating a life where you can truly thrive.

This journey has been deeply personal for me, rooted in my own struggles with burnout, the lessons I learned, and the insights I discovered along the way. It is not just my story. It is the story of so many of us, living in a world that often equates endless productivity with working harder and longer at the expense of our well-being. The reality is, burnout is not just an individual issue; it is a systemic problem that affects teams and entire organizations, limiting capacity, creativity, and ultimately preventing us from fully realizing our potential or achieving our missions.

The solution? Your *Elite Energy* system. It is not just a static tool. It is a dynamic, visual framework that breaks down the essential components of well-being, providing a clear, practical way to assess, address, and communicate your personal needs, so you can operate at your best.

At the base of your *Elite Energy* lies your personal *Values & Beliefs*, the foundation of your system and the bedrock upon which everything else is built. From there, we defined your *core*: *Mind*, *Body*, and *Heart*, the regular wellness practices and commitments necessary to support your mental, physical, and relational health. We also explored how you can best *Rest*—the practices that help you recharge and recover—and how you can *Reach*, setting stretch goals that challenge you to grow, build resilience, and expand your capacity.

Additionally, we discussed the importance of a *Purpose Statement* but emphasized that when you are in the midst of burnout, it is not the time to pressure yourself into defining your purpose. Instead, it is okay to rest, pause, reflect, and give yourself the space to explore who you want to be and what impact you wish to make. Finally, we looked at how all these elements work together as an ecosystem to create your *Elite Energy*, your overall well-being and best capacity.

As we explored how to put your system into practice, we learned that true impact comes from setting your rhythm, ensuring balance across your components, and adapting your system for the different seasons of your life. We also confronted the inevitability of setbacks and hardships. I shared how I leveraged the *Elite Energy* framework during my journey with cancer, demonstrating how this system can support you even in life's toughest moments.

Finally, we explored how applying this system is not only transformative for individuals, but also for teams and entire organizations. By prioritizing well-being in our workplaces and communities, we can shift the culture from one of burnout and exhaustion to one of sustainable growth, creativity, and collective flourishing.

THE NEXT STEP IN YOUR JOURNEY

As we close this book, I encourage you to move forward with courage and conviction in the commitments you have made throughout our time together. By doing so, you are paving the way for a future where your energy is intentionally cultivated, your potential unlocked, and your life is aligned with your values and purpose.

You have the power to make a profound difference, not only in your own life but in the lives of those around you. By committing to nurturing your *Elite Energy* system, you join a movement toward positive change; a movement that seeks to break the cycle of burnout, foster well-being, and create environments where people can thrive both personally and professionally.

The journey does not end here. It is ongoing and ever-evolving. Each step you take toward better understanding and managing your personal energy is a step toward greater health, happiness, and fulfillment. By investing in your *Elite Energy*, you are not simply surviving—you are actively choosing to thrive.

As we close, I leave you with this challenge: continue to invest in your *Elite Energy*. Prioritize your well-being. Honor your rhythm. Be honest about when you are ready to stretch beyond your comfort zone and when you need to recover. Above all, remain true to your values, beliefs, and purpose. In doing so, you are not just creating a life where you can thrive, you become an example for others to do the same.

The world needs your full energy, your best self.

Until next time,
Bree

ACKNOWLEDGMENTS

---

*"No one who achieves success does so without
the help of others. The wise and confident
acknowledge this help with gratitude."*

—ALFRED NORTH WHITEHEAD

This book would not exist without the love, patience, and support of my incredible husband, Neil Bacon. From the moment I began this journey of creating the *Elite Energy* concept to the final word written, you were there every step of the way. You not only believed in this project but in me. Especially during some of the hardest seasons of my life. Your strength, encouragement, and love have been a constant source of energy. I am beyond blessed to walk this crazy journey called life with you.

A heartfelt thank you to the entire Manuscripts LLC team. A special mention to my positioning specialist, Angela Murray; my development editor, Zach Marcum; and my revisions editor, Carol McKibben, for their invaluable contributions. Writing a book was never on my bucket list (and I would not call myself a writer), but thanks to all of you, I achieved something I did not know was possible.

I am profoundly thankful to my interviewees for generously sharing their stories and allowing me to incorporate their insights: Neil Bacon, Lieutenant Colonel Kurt Steinmetz, Mark Stern, Amara Falk, Dr. Jerome M. Adams, and Kara Hardin.

To all my beta readers who generously took the time and energy to read my book in its early and rough format, helping to shape it into what it is today, my deepest gratitude goes to: Amara Falk, Dave Henning, Dr. Christine Gilroy, Amy Bricker, Heidi Olson, Kasey Worrell, Barb Zeller, Brian Falk, Betty Falk, Elisa Knoepfel, Amy Dawson, Gavin Galimi, Emily Bohnemeier, and Mecca Williams.

Finally, thank you to my readers. I truly appreciate you taking the time to read my book. If you enjoyed the concept, I would be so grateful if you could leave a review and share it with a friend. Your support means the world to me. Thank you!

NOTES

INTRODUCTION: DID I MISS A CLASS?

1. Jen Fisher and Paul H. Silverglate, "The C-Suite's Role in Well-Being," *Deloitte Insights* (blog), June 22, 2022, https://www2.deloitte.com/us/en/insights/topics/leadership/employee-wellness-in-the-corporate-workplace.html.

2a. *Hybrid Work Is Just Work. Are We Doing It Wrong?* Work Trend Index Special Report (Redmond, Washington: Microsoft, September 22, 2022), https://www.microsoft.com/en-us/worklab/work-trend-index/hybrid-work-is-just-work.

2b. *Workforce 2.0: Unlocking Human Potential in a Machine-Augmented World—Global Talent Trends* (New York, New York: Mercer, March 11, 2024), 37, https://www.mercer.com/assets/global/en/shared-assets/local/attachments/pdf-2024-global-talent-trends-report-en.pdf.

3. World Health Organization, "Burn-out an 'Occupational Phenomenon': International Classification of Diseases," *Update* (Blog), May 28, 2019, https://www.who.int/news/item/28-05-2019-burn-out-an-occupational-phenomenon-international-classification-of-diseases.

4. Shana Lynch, "Why Your Workplace Might Be Killing You," *Insights* (blog), *Stanford Business School*, February 23, 2015, https://www.gsb.stanford.edu/insights/why-your-workplace-might-be-killing-you.

5a. *Britannica* (Chicago: Encyclopedia Britannica, Inc., 2024), s.v. "Energy," access date: December 6, 2024, https://www.britannica.com/science/energy.

5b. *Dictionary.com* (Long Beach, California: Lexico Publishing, 2024) s.v. "Elite," access date: December 6, 2024, https://www.dictionary.com/browse/elite#american-elite-adjective.

6. Saint Mary's University, "Newton's Cradle," *Classroom Physics Demos* (blog), *Saint Mary's University,* December 19, 2022, https://demos.smu.ca/demos/mechanics/136-newton-s-pendulum.

CHAPTER 1: CRASH AND BURN

1. Christina Maslach and Michael Leiter, *The Burnout Challenge: Managing People's Relationships with Their Jobs* (Cambridge, Massachusetts: Harvard University Press, 2022), 11.

2. Christina Maslach and Michael Leiter, *The Burnout Challenge: Managing People's Relationships with Their Jobs* (Cambridge, Massachusetts: Harvard University Press, 2022), 4.

3. *Britannica* (Chicago: Encyclopedia Britannica, Inc., 2024), s.v. "Energy," access date: December 6, 2024, https://www.britannica.com/science/energy.

CHAPTER 2: I AM NOT ALONE

1. Jim Harter, "Manager Burnout Is Only Getting Worse," *Workplace* (blog), *Gallup*, November 18, 2021, https://www.gallup.com/workplace/357404/manager-burnout-getting-worse.aspx.

2. American Psychological Association, "2023 Work in America Survey," n.d., access date: November 10, 2024, https://www.apa.org/pubs/reports/work-in-america/2023-workplace-health-well-being.

3. Ibid.

4. "Employers Need to Focus on Workplace Burnout: Here's Why," *Healthy Workplaces* (blog), *American Psychological Association,* May 12, 2023, https://www.apa.org/topics/healthy-workplaces/workplace-burnout.

5. Llewellyn E. van Zyl, "Is Burnout Making You Dumber?" *Burnout* (blog), *Psychology Today*, August 9, 2023, https://www.psychologytoday.com/us/blog/happybytes/202308/is-burnout-making-you-dumber.

6. Denise Salvagioni, Francine Melanda, Arthur Mesas, Alberto González, Flávia Gabani, and Selma Andrade, "Physical, Psychological and Occupational Consequences of Job Burnout: A Systematic Review of Prospective Studies," *PLoS ONE*, 12, 10 (October 2017): n.p., https://doi.org/10.1371/journal.pone.0185781.

7. Llewellyn E. van Zyl, "Is Burnout Making You Dumber?" *Burnout* (blog), *Psychology Today*, August 9, 2023, https://www.psychologytoday.com/us/blog/happybytes/202308/is-burnout-making-you-dumber.

8. Michael Precker, "How Job Burnout Can Hurt Your Health—and What to Do About It," *News* (blog), *American Heart Association News*, October 12, 2022, https://www.heart.org/en/news/2022/10/12/how-job-burnout-can-hurt-your-health-and-what-to-do-about-it.

9. Denise Salvagioni, Francine Melanda, Arthur Mesas, Alberto González, Flávia Gabani, and Selma Andrade, "Physical, Psychological and Occupational Consequences of Job Burnout: A Systematic Review of Prospective Studies," *PLoS ONE*, 12, 10 (October 2017): n.p., https://doi.org/10.1371/journal.pone.0185781.

10. Shana Lynch, "Why Your Workplace Might Be Killing You," *Insights* (blog), *Stanford Business School*, February 23, 2015, https://www.gsb.stanford.edu/insights/why-your-workplace-might-be-killing-you.

11. Michael Precker, "How Job Burnout Can Hurt Your Health—and What to Do About It," *News* (blog), *American Heart Association News*, October 12, 2022, https://www.heart.org/en/news/2022/10/12/how-job-burnout-can-hurt-your-health-and-what-to-do-about-it.

12. Alexandra Michel, "Burnout and the Brain," *Association for Psychological Science* (blog), January 29, 2016, https://www.psychologicalscience.org/observer/burnout-and-the-brain#:~:text=Those%20diagnosed%20with%20burnout%20reported,than%20did%20the%20control%20group.

13. Nicole K. McNichols, "How Burnout Can Affect Your Relationship," *Burnout* (blog), *Psychology Today*, December 8, 2021, https://www.psychologytoday.com/us/blog/everyone-on-top/202112/how-burnout-can-affect-your-relationship.

14. Lindsay Sears, Yuyan Shi,.Carter Coberley, and James Pope, "Overall Well-Being as a Predictor of Health Care, Productivity, and Retention Outcomes in a Large Employer," *Population Health Management* 16, no. 6 (December 2013): 397–405, https://pmc.ncbi.nlm.nih.gov/articles/PMC3870481/#abstract1.

15. Ibid

16. Aditi Nerurkar, Asaf Bitton, Roger Davis, Russell Phillips, Gloria Yeh, *When Physicians Counsel About Stress: Results of a National Study* (Chicago: JAMA Internal Medicine, January 14, 2013), https://jamanetwork.com/journals/jamainternalmedicine/fullarticle/1392494.

17. *2023 Employer Health Benefits Survey* (San Francisco, KFF, October 18, 2023), n.p., https://www.kff.org/report-section/ehbs-2023-summary-of-findings/#:~:text=AVAILABILITY%20OF%20EMPLOYER%2DSPONSORED%20COVERAGE&text=In%202023%2C%2053%25%20of%20all,percentage%20last-%20%20year%20(51%25).

18. Sunday Azagba and Mesbah Sharaf, *Psychosocial Working Conditions and the Utilization of Health Care Services* (Montreal, BMC Public Health, August 11, 2011), n.p., https://bmcpublichealth.biomedcentral.com/articles/10.1186/1471-2458-11-642.

19. Lindsay Sears, Yuyan Shi, Carter Coberley, and James Pope, "Overall Well-Being as a Predictor of Health Care, Productivity, and Retention Outcomes in a Large Employer," *Population Health Management* 16, no. 6 (December 2013): 397–405, https://pmc.ncbi.nlm.nih.gov/articles/PMC3870481/#abstract1.

20. "Health Care Costs: A Primer," *Health Costs* (blog), *KFF*, May 01, 2012, https://www.kff.org/health-costs/issue-brief/health-care-costs-a-primer/.

21. "NHE Fact Sheet, Centers for Medicare & Medicaid Services," *National Health Expenditures Data* (blog), *Center for Medicare and Medicaid Services*, access date: February 18, 2025, https://www.cms.gov/data-research/statistics-trends-and-reports/national-health-expenditure-data/nhe-fact-sheet.

22. *2024 Global Medical Trends Survey* (Dallas: WTW, November 28, 2023), https://www.wtwco.com/en-us/insights/2023/11/2024-global-medical-trends-survey.

23. Walter Stewart, Judith Ricci, Elsbeth Chee, and David Morganstein, "Lost Productive Work Time Costs from Health Conditions in the United States: Results From the American Productivity Audit," *Journal of Occupational and Environmental Medicine*, 45, no. 12, (December 2003): 1234–1236, https://journals.lww.com/joem/abstract/2003/12000/lost_productive_work_time_costs_from_health.4.aspx.

24. "Gallup Releases New Findings on the State of the American Workplace," *Gallup* (blog), June 11, 2013, https://news.gallup.com/opinion/gallup/170570/gallup-releases-new-findings-state-american-workplace.aspx.

25. "Employers Need to Focus on Workplace Burnout: Here's Why," *Burnout* (blog), *American Psychological Association*, May 12, 2023, https://www.apa.org/topics/healthy-workplaces/workplace-burnout.

26. Ibid.

27. *Employee Burnout in the Time of COVID-19: No Relief for Many Workers*, CHART Bulletin Series 16, Dec 2020, https://www.njha.com/media/619358/Employee-Burnout-Bulletin-COVID.pdf.

28. *State of the American Workplace* (Northwest New Mexico: Gallup, 2017), https://www.gallup.com/workplace/238085/state-american-workplace-report-2017.aspx?thank-you-report-form=1.

29. Kellie Hanna, *Employee Burnout Survey Finds 1 in 5 Workers Think About Quitting Their Job Daily* (San Francisco, California: My Perfect Resume, January 7, 2025), https://www.myperfectresume.com/career-center/careers/basics/worker-burnout.

30. Grace Sheppard, "When Vacations Aren't Enough: New Visier Survey Finds 70% of Burnt Out Employees Would Leave Current Job," *Future of Work* (blog), *Visier,* n.d., access date: December 1, 2024, https://www.visier.com/blog/new-survey-70-percent-burnt-out-employees-would-leave-current-job/.

31. American Psychological Association, "2023 Work in America Survey," n.d., access date: November 10, 2024, https://www.apa.org/pubs/reports/work-in-america/2023-workplace-health-well-being.

32. "Driving the Bottom Line: Improving Retention," *PricewaterhouseCoopers* (blog), 2006, https://www.shrm.org/content/dam/en/shrm/topics-tools/news/hr-magazine/saratoga-improving-retention.pdf.

33. Shane McFeely and Ben Wigert, "This Fixable Problem Costs US Businesses $1 Trillion," *Workplace* (blog), *Gallup*, March 13, 2019, https://www.gallup.com/workplace/247391/fixable-problem-costs-businesses-trillion.aspx.

34. "How Much Turnover Is Too Much?" *Mercer* (blog), September 05, 2024, https://www.imercer.com/articleinsights/workforce-turnover-trends#:~:text=The%20average%20turnover%20rate%20among%20US%20businesses,(4.8%)%2C%20where%20the%20company%20terminated%20the%20employee.

35. Jeffrey Pfeffer, *Dying for a Paycheck: How Modern Management Harms Employee Health and Company Performance—and What We Can Do About It* (New York: HarperCollins Publishers, 2018), 4.

CHAPTER 3: PROFESSOR PHYSICS

1. Julie Marks, "Grounding Exercises: Using Your 5 Senses for Anxiety Relief," *PsychCentral* (blog), October 8, 2021, https://psychcentral.com/anxiety/using-the-five-senses-for-anxiety-relief.

2. Saint Mary's University, "Newton's Cradle," *Classroom Physics Demos* (blog), *Saint Mary's University*, December 19, 2022, https://demos.smu.ca/demos/mechanics/136-newton-s-pendulum.

3. Yousef Haseli, "Conservation of Energy Principle," *ScienceDirect*, 2020, https://www.sciencedirect.com/topics/engineering/conservation-of-energy-principle#:~:text=The%20principle%20of%20energy%20conservation,it%20is%20an%20empirical%20law.

4. *Britannica* (Chicago: Encyclopedia Britannica, Inc., 2024), s.v. "Energy," access date: December 6, 2024, https://www.britannica.com/science/energy.

5. *Dictionary.com* (Long Beach, California: Lexico Publishing, 2024) s.v. "Elite," access date: December 6, 2024, https://www.dictionary.com/browse/elite#american-elite-adjective.

6. "Physical Health and Mental Health," *Explore Mental Health A to Z* (blog), *Mental Health Foundation,* February 18, 2022, https://www.mentalhealth.org.uk/explore-mental-health/a-z-topics/physical-health-and-mental-health#:~:text=Physical%20health%20problems%20significantly%20increase,most%20often%20depression%20or%20anxiety.

7. Elizabeth Perry, "Look to Your Social Health If You Want to Improve Your Well-Being," *Well Being* (blog), *BetterUp*, April 13, 2022, https://www.betterup.com/blog/what-is-social-health#:~:text=Good%20social%20health%20supports%20better,stress%2C%20and%20improved%20heart%20health.

8. US Department of Health and Human Services, "US Surgeon General Releases New Framework for Mental Health & Well-Being in the Workplace," October 20, 2022, https://www.hhs.gov/about/news/2022/10/20/us-surgeon-general-releases-new-framework-mental-health-well-being-workplace.html.

9. Tony Schwartz and Catherine McCarthy, "Manage Your Energy, Not Your Time," *Harvard Business Review*, October 2007, https://qualitycharters.org/wp-content/uploads/2016/05/HBR-Manage-Your-Energy.pdf.

10. *Workplace Well-Being Resources* (blog), *US Department of Health and Human Services*, August 2, 2024, https://www.hhs.gov/surgeongeneral/priorities/workplace-well-being/resources/index.html.

11. Ibid.

12. Bree Bacon, Bacon Enterprises L.L.C., January 2025, www.BreeBacon.com.

13. "The Small Steps That Have a Big Impact on Achieving Goals," *Health Care Management/Innovation* (blog), *Knowledge at Wharton*, January 12, 2015, https://knowledge.wharton.upenn.edu/article/small-steps-that-make-a-big-impact-on-achieving-goals/.

14. Shauna H. Springer, "What Works for Me May Not Work for You," *Career* (blog), *Psychology Today*, February 22, 2017, https://www.psychologytoday.com/intl/blog/free-range-psychology/201702/what-works-for-me-may-not-work-for-you.

CHAPTER 4: FOUNDATIONAL VALUES AND BELIEFS

1. "Comprehensive Airman Fitness Program," The High Rollers' Comprehensive Airman Fitness Program, 152nd Airlift Wing, access date: February 3, 2025, https://www.152aw.ang.af.mil/Members/Comprehensive-Airman-Fitness-Program/.

2. Christina Maslach and Michael P. Leiter, *The Burnout Challenge*, (Cambridge, Massachusetts and London, England: Harvard University Press, 2022), 157.

3. Adam M. Grant, "The Significance of Task Significance: Job Performance Effects, Relational Mechanisms, and Boundary Conditions," *Journal of Applied Psychology* 93, 1 (2008): 108–124, https://selfdeterminationtheory.org/SDT/documents/2008_Grant_JAP_TaskSignificance.pdf.

4. Viktor E. Frankl, *Man's Search for Meaning* (Boston, Massachusetts: Beacon Press, 1992), 46, https://antilogicalism.com/wp-content/uploads/2017/07/mans-search-for-meaning.pdf.

5. Viktor E. Frankl, *Man's Search for Meaning* (Boston, Massachusetts: Beacon Press, 1992), 5, https://antilogicalism.com/wp-content/uploads/2017/07/mans-search-for-meaning.pdf.

6. David Creswell, William Welch, Shelley Taylor, David Sherman, Tara Gruenewald, and Traci Mann, "Affirmation of Personal Values Buffers Neuroendocrine and Psychological Stress Responses," *Psychological Science* 16, 11, (2005): *846–851,* https://pubmed.ncbi.nlm.nih.gov/16262767/.

7. Carnegie Mellon University, "Self-affirmation Improves Problem-Solving Under Stress," *Science News* (blog), *ScienceDaily*, May 3,2013, www.sciencedaily.com/releases/2013/05/130503132956.htm.

8. *Encyclopedia Britannica 15th Edition* (Chicago: Encyclopedia Britannica, Inc., 2018) s.v. "15 Nelson Mandela Quotes," https://www.britannica.com/list/nelson-mandela-quotes.

9. Amira Najah, Abdulaziz Farooq, and Riadh Ben Rejeb, "Role of Religious Beliefs and Practices on the Mental Health of Athletes with Anterior Cruciate Ligament Injury," *Advances in Physical Education* 7, 2, (May 2017): 181–190, https://www.scirp.org/journal/paperinformation?paperid=76299.

10. René Hefti, "Integrating Religion and Spirituality into Mental Health Care, Psychiatry and Psychotherapy," *Religions* 2, 4, (December 2011): 611–627, https://www.mdpi.com/2077-1444/2/4/611.

11. Zahra Khiyali, Zeinab Naderi, Mohammadkazem Vakil, Hajar Ghasemi, Azizallah Dehghan, and Mostafa Bijani, "A Study of COVID-19 Anxiety, Spiritual Well-Being and Resilience Levels in Patients with Cancer Undergoing Chemotherapy during the COVID-19 Pandemic: a Cross-Sectional Study in the South of Iran," *BMC Psychology* 11, Article number: 75 (March 2023): https://bmcpsychology.biomedcentral.com/articles/10.1186/s40359-023-01126-1#citeas.

12. Amanda Howard, Megan Roberts, Tony Mitchell, and Nicole Wilke, "The Relationship Between Spirituality and Resilience and Well-being: a Study of 529 Care Leavers from 11 Nations," *Adversity and Resilience Science* 4, 2, (February 2023):177–190, https://pmc.ncbi.nlm.nih.gov/articles/PMC9918825/#:~:text=Data%20revealed%20 that%20spirituality%20was,Index%20scores%2C%20and%20childhood%20adversity.

13. Jonathan Hancock, "What Are Your Values?" *Personal Development* (blog), *Mindtools,* access date: December 17, 2024, https://www.mindtools.com/a5eygum/what-are-your-values.

CHAPTER 5: CORE I—MIND

1. "Mental Health," *Fact Sheets* (Blog), World Health Organization, June 17, 2022, https://www.who.int/news-room/fact-sheets/detail/mental-health-strengthening-our-response.

2. Mind Share Partners, "New Poll: Stress About Mental Health Is an Obstacle to Productivity at Work," *Mind Share Partners* (Blog), April 30, 2024, https://www.mindsharepartners.org/blog/mind-share-partners-harris-poll-on-state-of-employee-wellbeing.

3. US Department of Health and Human Services, "Workplace Mental Health and Well-Being," *Office of the Surgeon General* (Blog), access date: December 19, 2024, https://www.hhs.gov/surgeongeneral/priorities/workplace-well-being/index.html.

4. Llewellyn E. van Zyl, "Is Burnout Making You Dumber?" *Psychology Today,* August 9, 2023, https://www.psychologytoday.com/us/blog/happybytes/202308/is-burnout-making-you-dumber.

5. Ibid.

6. Vincent Kim Seng Oh, Abdullah Sarwar, and Niaz Pervez, "The Study of Mindfulness as an Intervening Factor for Enhanced Psychological Well-being in Building the Level of Resilience," *Frontiers in Psychology,* 13, (2022): n.p., https://doi.org/10.3389/fpsyg.2022.1056834.

7. Adrianna MacPherson, "How to Build Resilience and Boost your Mental Health," *Health And Wellness/Society and Culture* (blog), *University of Alberta,* January 26, 2022, https://www.ualberta.ca/en/folio/2022/01/how-to-build-resilience-and-boost-your-mental-health.html.

8. Marla Kauffman, "The Power of Gratitude: A Scientific Look at How Thankfulness Boosts Mental Health," *Addiction* (blog), *Institute for Research, Education & Training in Addictions,* December 20, 2023, https://ireta.org/the-power-of-gratitude-a-scientific-look-at-how-thankfulness-boosts-mental-health/#:~:text=Gratitude%20and%20 Brain%20Function&text=The%20findings%20revealed%20heightened%20 activity,regulation%20and%20decision%2Dmaking%20skills.

9. Elizabeth Hopper, "Four Ways Gratitude Helps You with Difficult Feelings," *Greater Good Magazine*, November 19, 2019, https://greatergood.berkeley.edu/article/item/four_ways_gratitude_helps_you_with_difficult_feelings.

10. Jeremy Sutton, "5 Benefits of Journaling for Mental Health," *Stress & Burnout Prevention* (blog), *PositivePsychology.com*, May 14, 2018, https://positivepsychology.com/benefits-of-journaling/.

11. Ibid.

12. Better Health, "Thought Record," *Mental wellbeing tips/Self-Help CBT Technologies* (blog), access date: December 19, 2024, https://www.nhs.uk/every-mind-matters/mental-wellbeing-tips/self-help-cbt-techniques/thought-record/#:~:text=A%20thought%20record%20is%20a%20common%20cognitive,and%20behaviours%20can%20be%2C%20and%20how%20they.

13. Mayo Clinic Staff, "Mindfulness exercises," *Consumer Health* (blog), October 11, 2022, https://www.mayoclinic.org/healthy-lifestyle/consumer-health/in-depth/mindfulness-exercises/art-20046356.

14. Sarah Garone, "8 Physical and Mental Health Benefits of Silence, Plus How to Get More of It," *Healthline* (blog), September 24, 2021, https://www.healthline.com/health/mind-body/physical-and-mental-health-benefits-of-silence.

15. "Taking Breaks," *The Learning Center* (blog), *The University of North Carolina at Chapel Hill,* access date: December 19, 2024, https://learningcenter.unc.edu/tips-and-tools/taking-breaks/.

16. Lawrence Robinson, Melinda Smith, Jeanne Segal, and Jennifer Shubin, "The Benefits of Play for Adults," *Well-being & Happiness* (blog), *HelpGuide*, access date: December 19, 2024, https://www.helpguide.org/mental-health/wellbeing/benefits-of-play-for-adults.

17. "Happy workers are 13% more productive," *News & Events* (blog), *University of Oxford,* October 24, 2019, https://www.ox.ac.uk/news/2019-10-24-happy-workers-are-13-more-productive.

18. Todd Hollingshead, "Study: Collaborative video games could increase office productivity," *Intellect* (blog), *BYU*, January 28, 2019, https://news.byu.edu/news/study-collaborative-video-games-could-increase-office-productivity.

19. Smitha Bhandari, "Setting Boundaries," Mental Health (blog), *WebMD*, February 25, 2024, https://www.webmd.com/mental-health/setting-boundaries.

20. Bree Bacon, Bacon Enterprises L.L.C., January 2025, www.BreeBacon.com.

CHAPTER 6: CORE II—BODY

1 Virginia Wesleyan University, "Health & Wellness: Physical Health," *Research Guides* (blog), *H.C. Hofheimer,* December 12, 2024, https://guides.vwu.edu/c.php?g=20994&p=122669.

2. Valerie Bolden-Barrett, "Poor Mental, Physical Health Carry Significant Risk for Productivity Loss," *Dive Brief* (blog), *HRDive*, June 14, 2019, https://www.hrdive.com/news/poor-mental-physical-health-carry-significant-risk-for-productivity-loss/556689/.

3. Debra Fulghum Bruce, "Exercise and Depression: How Physical Activity Can Help," *Depression* (blog), *WebMD*, February 9, 2025, https://www.webmd.com/depression/exercise-depression.

4. Excel Psychiatry, "The Importance of Sleep to Your Physical and Emotional Health," *Mental Health* (blog), access date: December 24, 2024, https://excel-psychiatry.com/importance-of-sleep-for-physical-and-emotional-health/#:~:text=Prioritizing%20sleep%20is%20a%20proactive,to%20assess%20situations%20with%20clarity.

5. Laura Lachance and Drew Ramsey, "Food, Mood, and Brain Health: Implications for the Modern Clinician," *Missouri Medicine* 12, 2, (March–April 2015): 111–115, https://pmc.ncbi.nlm.nih.gov/articles/PMC6170050/.

6. Tinh Doan, Van Ha, Lyndall Strazdins, and Dan Chateau, "Healthy Minds Live in Healthy Bodies—Effect of Physical Health on Mental Health: Evidence from Australian Longitudinal Data," *Current Psychology* 42, (2023): 18702–18713, https://link.springer.com/article/10.1007/s12144-022-03053-7.

7. Centers for Disease Control, "Physical Activity Boosts Brain Health," *Physical Activity* (blog), January 31, 2025, https://www.cdc.gov/physical-activity/features/boost-brain-health.html?CDC_AAref_Val=https://www.cdc.gov/nccdphp/dnpao/features/physical-activity-brain-health/index.html.

8. Harvard Health Publishing, "Exercising to Relax," *Staying Healthy* (blog), *Harvard Medical School*, July 7, 2020, https://www.health.harvard.edu/staying-healthy/exercising-to-relax.

9. Matheus Santos de Sousa Fernandes, Tayrine Figueira Ordônio, Gabriela Carvalho Jurema Santos, Lucas Eduardo R Santos, Camila Tenório Calazans, Dayane Aparecida Gomes, and Tony Meireles Santos, "Effects of Physical Exercise on Neuroplasticity and Brain Function: A Systematic Review in Human and Animal Studies," *Neural Plasticity* 2020, (December 2020): 8856621, https://pmc.ncbi.nlm.nih.gov/articles/PMC7752270/.

10. American Psychological Association, "Stress and Sleep," 2013, https://www.apa.org/news/press/releases/stress/2013/sleep#:~:text=6,point%20scale)%20say%20the%20same.

11. Marni N. Silverman and Patricia A. Deuster, "Biological Mechanisms Underlying the Role of Physical Fitness in Health and Resilience," *The Royal Society*, 4, 5 (October 2014): n.p., https://doi.org/10.1098/rsfs.2014.0040.

12. Harriett Neverdon, "A New Prescription: Treating Disease with Exercise," *Health & Wellness* (blog), *Maryland Primary Care Physicians*, access date: December 26, 2024, https://www.mpcp.com/articles/healthy-lifestyle/a-new-prescription-treating-disease-with-exercise/.

13. Mamata Yadav, "Diet, Sleep and Exercise: The Keystones of Healthy Lifestyle for Medical Students," *Journal of the Nepal Medical Association* 60, 253, (September 2022): 841-843, https://pmc.ncbi.nlm.nih.gov/articles/PMC9794932/.

14. Laura Lachance and Drew Ramsey, "Food, Mood, and Brain Health: Implications for the Modern Clinician," *Missouri Medicine* 112, 2 (2015): 111-5, https://pmc.ncbi.nlm.nih.gov/articles/PMC6170050/.

15. Ibid.

16. Rob Newsom and Anis Rehman, "The Connection Between Diet, Exercise, and Sleep," *Physical Sleep and Health* (blog), *SleepFoundation*, April 1, 2024, https://www.sleepfoundation.org/physical-health/diet-exercise-sleep#references-183428.

17. Chioma J Ikonte, Jonathan G Mun, Carroll A Reider, Ryan W Grant, and Susan Hazels Mitmesser, "Micronutrient Inadequacy in Short Sleep: Analysis of the NHANES 2005-2016." *Nutrients* 11, 10 (2019): 2335, https://doi.org/10.3390/nu11102335.

18. Harvard University Health Services, "Physical," *Your Wellbeing* (blog), *Center for Wellness and Health Promotion*, access date: December 26, 2024, https://wellness.huhs.harvard.edu/physical.

19. World Health Organization, "Healthy Diet," *Fact Sheets* (blog), April 29, 2020, https://www.who.int/news-room/fact-sheets/detail/healthy-diet.

20. Whitney Hopler, "Famous Quotes on Nutrition and Well-Being," *Center for the Advancement of Well-being* (blog), *George Mason University*, access date: December 26, 2024, https://wellbeing.gmu.edu/famous-quotes-on-nutrition-and-well-being/.

21. Daniel McDonald, et al., "American Gut: an Open Platform for Citizen Science Microbiome Research," *mSystems* 3, 3 (May 2018): 1128, https://doi.org/10.1128/msystems.00031-18.

22. Mayo Clinic Staff, "Water: How Much Should You Drink Every Day?" *Healthy Lifestyle* (blog), *Mayo Clinic*, access date: December 26, 2024, https://www.mayoclinic.org/healthy-lifestyle/nutrition-and-healthy-eating/in-depth/water/art-20044256#:~:text=So%20how%20much%20fluid%20does,fluids%20a%20day%20for%20women.

23. Whitney Hopler, "Famous Quotes on Nutrition and Well-Being," *Center for the Advancement of Well-being* (blog), *George Mason University*, access date: December 26, 2024, https://wellbeing.gmu.edu/famous-quotes-on-nutrition-and-well-being/.

24. "Good News: You Can Make Up for Lost Sleep Over the Weekend (Kind Of)," *healthessentials* (blog), *Cleveland Clinic*, August 15, 2023, https://health.clevelandclinic.org/insomnia-can-you-make-up-for-lost-sleep-on-weekends.

25. Yong Liu, Anne G Wheaton, Daniel P Chapman, Timothy J Cunningham, Hua Lu, and Janet B Croft, "Prevalence of Healthy Sleep Duration among Adults--United States, 2014," *Morbidity and Mortality Weekly Report* 65, 6, (February 2016): 137–141, https://doi.org/10.15585/mmwr.mm6506a1.

26. Eric Suni and Ealena Callender, "What Happens When You Sleep?" *How Sleep Works* (blog), *SleepFoundation*, December 22, 2023, https://www.sleepfoundation.org/how-sleep-works/what-happens-when-you-sleep.

27. Harvard Medical School, "Why Sleep Matters: Consequences of Sleep Deficiency," *Education and Training* (blog), *Division of Sleep Medicine*, October 1, 2021, https://sleep.hms.harvard.edu/education-training/public-education/sleep-and-health-education-program/sleep-health-education-45.

28. "More Sleep Would Make Us Happier, Healthier, And Safer," *Psychology Topics* (blog), *American Psychological Association*, 2014, https://www.apa.org/topics/sleep/deprivation-consequences.

29. Eric Suni and Abhinav Singh, "How Much Sleep Do You Need?" *How Sleep Works* (blog), *SleepFoundation*, May 13, 2024, https://www.sleepfoundation.org/how-sleep-works/how-much-sleep-do-we-really-need.

30. Mayo Clinic Staff, "Sleep Tips: 6 Steps to Better Sleep," *Healthy Lifestyle* (blog), *Mayo Clinic*, access date: December 26, 2024, https://www.mayoclinic.org/healthy-lifestyle/adult-health/in-depth/sleep/art-20048379.

31. Eric Suni and Abhinav Singh, "How Much Sleep Do You Need?" *How Sleep Works* (blog), *SleepFoundation*, May 13, 2024, https://www.sleepfoundation.org/how-sleep-works/how-much-sleep-do-we-really-need.

32. Mayo Clinic Staff, "Sleep tips: 6 Steps to Better Sleep," *Healthy Lifestyle* (blog), *Mayo Clinic*, access date: December 26, 2024, https://www.mayoclinic.org/healthy-lifestyle/adult-health/in-depth/sleep/art-20048379.

33. "Physical Activity," *Fact Sheets* (blog), *World Health Organization,* June 26, 2024, https://www.who.int/news-room/fact-sheets/detail/physical-activity.

34. Frank W. Booth, Christian K. Roberts, and Matthew J. Laye, "Lack of Exercise Is a Major Cause of Chronic Diseases," *Comprehensive Physiology* 2, 2, (April 2012): n.p., https://doi.org/10.1002/cphy.c110025.

35. John D. Omura, David R. Brown, Lisa C. McGuire, Christopher A. Taylor, Janet E. Fulton, and Susan A. Carlson, "Cross-Sectional Association Between Physical Activity Level and Subjective Cognitive Decline among US Adults Aged ≥45 years, 2015," *Preventive Medicine* 141, (2020): 106279, https://doi.org/10.1016/j.ypmed.2020.106279.

36. Hannah Steinberg, Elizabeth A Sykes, Tim Moss, Susan Lowery, Nick LeBoutillier, and Alison Dewey, "Exercise Enhances Creativity Independently of Mood," *British Journal of Sports Medicine* 31, 3 (1997): https://bjsm.bmj.com/content/31/3/240.

37. "Physical Activity," *Fact Sheets* (blog), *World Health Organization,* June 26, 2024, https://www.who.int/news-room/fact-sheets/detail/physical-activity.

38. Howard E. LeWine, "Exercise and Fitness," *Harvard Health Publishing* (blog), September 27, 2024, https://www.health.harvard.edu/topics/exercise-and-fitness.

39. Leadership Now, "Quotes about INITIATIVE," *Leading Thoughts*, access date: December 24, 2024, https://leadershipnow.com/initiativequotes.html.

40. Bree Bacon, Bacon Enterprises L.L.C., January 2025, www.BreeBacon.com.

CHAPTER 7: CORE III—HEART

1. US Department of Health & Human Services, *Our Epidemic of Loneliness and Isolation,* (Washington, D.C.: US Surgeon General, 2023), 10, https://www.hhs.gov/sites/default/files/surgeon-general-social-connection-advisory.pdf.

2. Ibid.

3. Karmel W. Choi, et al., "An Exposure-Wide and Mendelian Randomization Approach to Identifying Modifiable Factors for the Prevention of Depression," *American Journal of Psychiatry* 177, 10, (October 2020): 944–54, https://psychiatryonline.org/doi/10.1176/appi.ajp.2020.19111158.

4. Julianne Holt-Lunstad, Timothy B. Smith, J. Bradley Layton, "Social Relationships and Mortality Risk: A Meta-analytic Review," *PLoS Med* 7, 7, (July 2010): n.p., https://doi.org/10.1371/journal.pmed.1000316.

5. Zara Abrams, "The Science of Why Friendships Keep Us Healthy," *American Psychological Association* 54, 4 (June 1, 2023): https://www.apa.org/monitor/2023/06/cover-story-science-friendship.

6. Vivek H. Murthy, "Column: US Surgeon General: Loneliness Is at Heart of Growing Mental Health Crisis," *U Magazine*, June 29, 2023, https://www.uclahealth.org/news/publication/column-us-surgeon-general-loneliness-heart-growing-mental.

7. US Department of Health & Human Services, *Our Epidemic of Loneliness and Isolation,* (Washington, D.C.: US Surgeon General, 2023), 23, https://www.hhs.gov/sites/default/files/surgeon-general-social-connection-advisory.pdf.

8. Steve Cole, "Social Regulation of Human Gene Expression," *Current Directions in Psychological Science*, 18, 3 (2009): 132–137. https://pmc.ncbi.nlm.nih.gov/articles/PMC3020789/#:~:text=Several%20studies%20have%20shown%20that,et%20al.%2C%202007).

9. Nicole K Valtorta, et al. "Loneliness and Social Isolation as Risk Factors for Coronary Heart Disease and Stroke: Systematic Review and Meta-Analysis of Longitudinal Observational Studies." *Heart* (British Cardiac Society) 102, 13 (2016): 1009–16. https://heart.bmj.com/content/102/13/1009.

10. Stephanie Brinkhues, et al. "Socially Isolated Individuals Are More Prone to Have Newly Diagnosed and Prevalent Type 2 Diabetes Mellitus—The Maastricht Study," *BMC Public Health* 17, 1 (December 2017): 955, https://pmc.ncbi.nlm.nih.gov/articles/PMC5735891/#Sec21.

11. US Department of Health & Human Services, *Our Epidemic of Loneliness and Isolation,* (Washington, D.C.: US Surgeon General, 2023), 25, https://www.hhs.gov/sites/default/files/surgeon-general-social-connection-advisory.pdf.

12. Yang Claire Yang, et al. "Social Relationships and Physiological Determinants of Longevity Across the Human Life Span." *Proceedings of the National Academy of Sciences of the United States of America*, 113, 3 (2016): 578–83, https://www.pnas.org/doi/full/10.1073/pnas.1511085112.

13. Sheldon Cohen, "Psychosocial Vulnerabilities to Upper Respiratory Infectious Illness: Implications for Susceptibility to Coronavirus Disease 2019 (COVID-19)," *Perspectives on Psychological Science* 16, 1, (2021): 161–174, https://doi.org/10.1177/1745691620942516.

14. US Department of Health & Human Services, *Our Epidemic of Loneliness and Isolation,* (Washington, D.C.: US Surgeon General, 2023), 24, https://www.hhs.gov/sites/default/files/surgeon-general-social-connection-advisory.pdf.

15. Ibid.

16. US Department of Health & Human Services, *Our Epidemic of Loneliness and Isolation,* (Washington, D.C.: US Surgeon General, 2023), 4, https://www.hhs.gov/sites/default/files/surgeon-general-social-connection-advisory.pdf.

17. US Department of Health & Human Services, *Our Epidemic of Loneliness and Isolation,* (Washington, D.C.: US Surgeon General, 2023), 28, https://www.hhs.gov/sites/default/files/surgeon-general-social-connection-advisory.pdf.

18. Laura Silver, Patrick van Kessel, Christine Huang, Laura Clancy, and Sneha Gubbala, *What Makes Life Meaningful? Views From 17 Advanced Economies* (Washington, D.C.: Pew Research Center, November 18, 2021): n.p., https://www.pewresearch.org/global/2021/11/18/what-makes-life-meaningful-views-from-17-advanced-economies/.

19. Steven M Southwick, et al, "Why Are Some Individuals More Resilient Than Others: The Role of Social Support." *World Psychiatry* 15, 1 (2016): 77–9. https://onlinelibrary.wiley.com/doi/10.1002/wps.20282.

20. Elizabeth Hopper, "Four Ways Gratitude Helps You with Difficult Feelings," *Relationships* (blog), *Greater Good Magazine*, November 19, 2019, https://greatergood.berkeley.edu/article/item/four_ways_gratitude_helps_you_with_difficult_feelings.

21. US Department of Health & Human Services, *Our Epidemic of Loneliness and Isolation,* (Washington, D.C.: US Surgeon General, 2023), 34, https://www.hhs.gov/sites/default/files/surgeon-general-social-connection-advisory.pdf.

22. Ibid.

23. US Department of Health & Human Services, *Our Epidemic of Loneliness and Isolation,* (Washington, D.C.: US Surgeon General, 2023), 34, https://www.hhs.gov/sites/default/files/surgeon-general-social-connection-advisory.pdf.

24. US Department of Health & Human Services, *Our Epidemic of Loneliness and Isolation,* (Washington, D.C.: US Surgeon General, 2023), 4, https://www.hhs.gov/sites/default/files/surgeon-general-social-connection-advisory.pdf.

25. US Department of Health & Human Services, *Our Epidemic of Loneliness and Isolation,* (Washington, D.C.: US Surgeon General, 2023), 9, https://www.hhs.gov/sites/default/files/surgeon-general-social-connection-advisory.pdf.

26. David L DuBois, Nelson Portillo, Jean E Rhodes, Naida Silverthorn, and Jeffrey C Valentine, "How Effective Are Mentoring Programs for Youth? A Systematic Assessment of the Evidence," *Psychological Science in the Public Interest* 12, 2, (2011): 57–91. https://doi.org/10.1177/1529100611414806.

27. Christopher Spera, et al, "Out of Work? Volunteers Have Higher Odds of Getting Back to Work," *Nonprofit and Voluntary Sector Quarterly* 44, 5, (2015): 886–907. https://doi.org/10.1177/0899764015605928.

28. Veronica Boswell and Carly Collins, "How to Put Your Phone Down and Be Present," *Healthy Living* (blog), *Tallahassee Memorial Healthcare*, March 10, 2023, https://www.tmh.org/healthy-living/blogs/healthy-living/how-to-put-your-phone-down-and-be-present.

29. US Department of Health & Human Services, *Our Epidemic of Loneliness and Isolation,* (Washington, D.C.: US Surgeon General, 2023), 19–20, https://www.hhs.gov/sites/default/files/surgeon-general-social-connection-advisory.pdf.

30. Ibid.

31. Michael Gingerich and Tom Kaden, "The Power of His Voice," *Someone To Tell It To* (blog), May 11, 2023, https://www.someonetotellitto.org/blog/the-power-of-his-voice.

32. Ibid.

33. US Department of Health & Human Services, *Our Epidemic of Loneliness and Isolation,* (Washington, D.C.: US Surgeon General, 2023), 5, https://www.hhs.gov/sites/default/files/surgeon-general-social-connection-advisory.pdf.

34. US Department of Health & Human Services, *Our Epidemic of Loneliness and Isolation,* (Washington, D.C.: US Surgeon General, 2023), 16, https://www.hhs.gov/sites/default/files/surgeon-general-social-connection-advisory.pdf.

35. Ibid.

36. US Department of Health & Human Services, *Our Epidemic of Loneliness and Isolation,* (Washington, D.C.: US Surgeon General, 2023), 38, https://www.hhs.gov/sites/default/files/surgeon-general-social-connection-advisory.pdf.

37. Ricky N. Lawton, et al, "Does Volunteering Make Us Happier, or Are Happier People More Likely to Volunteer? Addressing the Problem of Reverse Causality When Estimating the Wellbeing Impacts of Volunteering," *J Happiness Stud* 22, (2021): 599–624, https://link.springer.com/article/10.1007/s10902-020-00242-8.

38. Ashley Abramson, "Cultivating Empathy," *Monitor on Psychology* 52, 8 (2021): 44, https://www.apa.org/monitor/2021/11/feature-cultivating-empathy.

39. Naomi Brower, "Effective Communication Skills: Resolving Conflicts," *Relationships* (blog), *Utah State University,* access date: December 31, 2024, https://extension.usu.edu/relationships/research/effective-communication-skills-resolving-conflicts.

40. Ibid.

41. Naomi Brower, "Effective Communication Skills: Resolving Conflicts," *Relationships* (blog), *Utah State University,* access date: December 31, 2024, https://extension.usu.edu/relationships/research/effective-communication-skills-resolving-conflicts.

42. Bree Bacon, Bacon Enterprises L.L.C., January 2025, www.BreeBacon.com.

CHAPTER 8: REST AND REACH

1. Rick Ansorge, "Rest and Recovery Are Critical For An Athlete's Physiological and Psychological Well-being," *UCHealth Today* (blog), February 7, 2022, https://www.uchealth.org/today/rest-and-recovery-for-athletes-physiological-psychological-well-being/.

2. Amy Novotney, "The Science of Creativity," *gradPSYCH Magazine* 7, 1 (2009): 14, https://www.apa.org/gradpsych/2009/01/creativity.

3. Ibid.

4. Kimerer L. LaMothe, "Three Reasons to Move to the Beat," *Working Knowledge, Psychology Today,* February 13, 2023, https://www.psychologytoday.com/us/blog/what-a-body-knows/202302/three-reasons-to-move-to-the-beat.

5. Ibid.

6. Hancock Health, "5 Reasons Why Downtime Is Important," *Wellness* (blog), January 12, 2023, https://www.hancockhealth.org/2023/01/5-reasons-why-downtime-is-important/.

7. Cleveland Clinic, "Why Downtime Is Essential for Brain Health," *HealthEssentials* (blog), June 2, 2020, https://health.clevelandclinic.org/why-downtime-is-essential-for-brain-health.

8. Ibid.

9. Mia Primeau, "Your Powerful, Changeable Mindset," *Health & Medicine* (blog), *Stanford Report,* September 15, 2021, https://news.stanford.edu/stories/2021/09/mindsets-clearing-lens-life.

10. Ibid.

11. US Public Health Services, "The US Surgeon General's Framework for Workplace Mental Health & Well-Being," 2022, https://www.hhs.gov/sites/default/files/workplace-mental-health-well-being.pdf.

12. Marissa A. Sharif, Cassie Mogilner, and Hal E. Hershfield, "Having Too Little or Too Much Time Is Linked to Lower Subjective Well-Being," *Journal of Personality and Social Psychology* 121, 4, (2021): 933–947, https://doi.org/10.1037/pspp0000391.

13. Bree Bacon, Bacon Enterprises L.L.C., January 2025, www.BreeBacon.com.

CHAPTER 9: PURPOSE STATEMENT

1. Zameena Mejia, "Harvard Researchers Say This Mental Shift Will Help You Live a Longer, Healthier Life," *Leadership* (blog), *CNBC,* November 21, 2017, https://www.cnbc.com/2017/11/21/harvard-researchers-say-a-purpose-leads-to-longer-healthier-life.html.

2. "Purpose in Life Can Lead to Less Stress, Better Mental Well-being," *APA Blogs* (blog), *American Psychiatric Association,* December 7, 2023, https://www.psychiatry.org/news-room/apa-blogs/purpose-in-life-less-stress-better-mental-health.

3. Rosean Bishop, "Does Purpose Play a Positive Role in Mental Health?" *Speaking of Health* (blog), *Mayo Clinic Health System,* March 15, 2023, https://www.mayoclinichealthsystem.org/hometown-health/speaking-of-health/purpose-and-mental-health.

4. Eric S. Kim, Ying Chen, Julia S. Nakamura, Carol D. Ryff, and Tyler J. VanderWeele, "Sense of Purpose in Life and Subsequent Physical, Behavioral, and Psychosocial Health: An Outcome-Wide Approach," *American Journal of Health Promotion* 36, 1 (2022): 137–147, https://pmc.ncbi.nlm.nih.gov/articles/PMC8669210/.

5. "2023 Work in America Survey," *Reports/Work in America* (blog), *American Psychological Association,* access date: January 4, 2025, https://www.apa.org/pubs/reports/work-in-america/2023-workplace-health-well-being.

6. Sarah Greenberg, "The Importance of Living a Purpose-Driven Life," *Meaning* (blog), *VIA Institute on Character,* access date: January 4, 2025, https://www.viacharacter.org/topics/articles/the-importance-of-living-a-purpose-driven-life.

7. Bree Bacon, Bacon Enterprises L.L.C., January 2025, www.BreeBacon.com.

CHAPTER 10: RHYTHM, BALANCE, AND SEASONS

1. Chris Schulz, "How Newton's Cradles Work," *Inventions* (blog), *HowStuffsWorks,* access date: January 6, 2025, https://science.howstuffworks.com/innovation/inventions/newtons-cradle.htm.

2. Ibid.

3. Sujana Reddy, Vamsi Reddy, and Sandeep Sharma, "Physiology, Circadian Rhythm," *StatPearls Publishing,* May 1, 2023, https://www.ncbi.nlm.nih.gov/books/NBK519507/.

4. Ewa A Miendlarzewska and Wiebke J Trost, "How Musical Training Affects Cognitive Development: Rhythm, Reward and Other Modulating Variables." *Frontiers in Neuroscience* 7, (January 2014): 279, https://pmc.ncbi.nlm.nih.gov/articles/PMC3957486/.

5. Brad Stulberg, "7 Quotes on Sustainable Peak Performance That Everyone Needs to Read and Know," LinkedIn, accessed March 3, 2025, https://www.linkedin.com/posts/brad-stulberg-009b168b_7-quotes-on-sustainable-peak-performance-activity-7049724523981520896-05NW/.

6. "Why Routines Are Good for Your Health," *Living Real Change* (blog), *Piedmont,* access date: January 6, 2025, https://www.piedmont.org/living-real-change/why-routines-are-good-for-your-health#:~:text=Benefits%20of%20routines,day%20and%20subsequently%2C%20your%20life.

7. "Health Benefits of Having a Routine," *HealthBeat* (blog), *Northwestern Medicine,* December 2022, https://www.nm.org/healthbeat/healthy-tips/health-benefits-of-having-a-routine.

8. University of Florida, "Adding Variety To An Exercise Routine Helps Increase Adherence," October 24, 2000, https://archive.news.ufl.edu/articles/2000/10/adding-variety-to-an-exercise-routine-helps-increase-adherence.html.

9. Chris Schulz, "How Newton's Cradles Work," *Inventions* (blog), *HowStuffsWorks,* access date: January 6, 2025, https://science.howstuffworks.com/innovation/inventions/newtons-cradle.htm.

CHAPTER 11: WHEN LIFE GETS HARD

1. Naomi Breslau and Ronald Kessler, "The Stressor Criterion in DSM-IV Posttraumatic Stress Disorder: An Empirical Investigation," *Biological Psychiatry* 50, 9, (2001): 699–704, https://www.researchgate.net/publication/11650812_The_stressor_criterion_in_DSM-IV_Posttraumatic_Stress_Disorder_An_empirical_investigation.

2. "Trauma," *Psychological Topics* (blog), *American Psychological Association*, n.d., access date: February 17, 2025, https://www.apa.org/topics/trauma.

3. "Understanding Trauma and PTSD," *Mental Health America,* n.d., access date: February 19, 2025, https://www.mhanational.org/understanding-trauma-and-ptsd.

4. "Trauma Response: Understanding How Trauma Affects Everyone Differently," *Mental Health* (blog), *University of Maryland Medical System*, n.d., access date: February 18, 2025, https://health.umms.org/2022/06/08/trauma-response/.

5. 1 Kings 19:11-12 (New International Version).

6. Becky Brasfield, "How to Move Forward After Going through a Crisis," *NAMI* (blog), *National Alliance On Mental Illness*, January 21, 2020, https://www.nami.org/recovery/how-to-move-forward-after-going-through-a-crisis/.

7. Howard E. LeWine, "Understanding the Stress Response," *Staying Healthy* (blog), *Harvard Health Publishing, Harvard Medical School*, April 3, 2024, https://www.health.harvard.edu/staying-healthy/understanding-the-stress-response.

8. Chelsea Long, "How the Parasympathetic Nervous System Can Lower Stress," *Health* (blog), *HSS*, August 30, 2021, https://www.hss.edu/article_parasympathetic-nervous-system.asp#:~:text=There%20are%20many%20ways%20to,what%20helps%20you%20to%20decompress.

9. Bessel van der Kolk, *The Body Keeps The Score: Brain, Mind, and Body in The Healing of Trauma* (New York: Penguin Books, 2015), 206–210.

10. Ibid.

CHAPTER 12: CREATING A CULTURE

1. "The Power of Accountability Partners," *Company/Industry* (blog), *Better You*, 2024, https://www.betteryou.ai/the-power-of-accountability-partners/#:~:text=The%20Effectiveness,have%20that%20accountability%20partner%20around.

2. Ibid.

3. Tony Schwartz and Catherine McCarthy, "Manage Your Energy, Not Your Time," *Harvard Business Review*, October 2007, https://qualitycharters.org/wp-content/uploads/2016/05/HBR-Manage-Your-Energy.pdf.

4. *Workplace Well-Being Resources* (blog), *US Department of Health and Human Services*, August 2, 2024, https://www.hhs.gov/surgeongeneral/priorities/workplace-well-being/resources/index.html.

5. Ibid.

6. Gettysburg College, "One Third of Your Life Is Spent at Work," n.d., access date: January 19, 2025, https://www.gettysburg.edu/news/stories?id=79db7b34-630c-4f49-ad32-4ab9ea48e72b#:~:text=Writer%20Annie%20Dillard%20famously%20said,on%20your%20quality%20of%20life.

7. Rebecca Noori, "The State of Workplace Connection in 2025: How Sociable Is Your Team?" *Employee Engagement* (blog), *Nectar*, February 10, 2025, https://nectarhr.com/blog/workplace-connection-statistics.

8. Ruth D'Alessandro, "Employee Engagement at Work: Definition and Guide," *Experience Management* (blog), *Qualtrics*, n.d., access date: January 19, 2025, https://www.qualtrics.com/en-au/experience-management/employee/employee-engagement/#:~:text=Increased%20revenue%20%E2%80%93%20according%20to%20Gallup,better%20business%20outcomes%20all%20round.

9. Ibid.

10. Bree Bacon, Bacon Enterprises L.L.C., January 2025, www.BreeBacon.com.

11. Ibid.

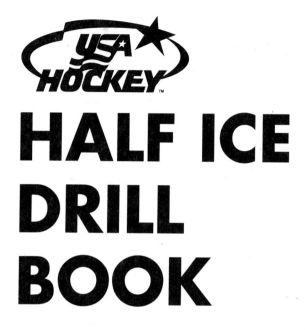

HALF ICE
DRILL
BOOK

Written for the USA Hockey
Coaching Education Program by:
    Val Belmonte
    Gary Gregus

Revised by:
    Mark Tabrum

The USA Hockey Coaching Education Program is presented by.

First printing 1997.

Library of Congress Cataloging in Publication Data:

Belmonte, Val , 1951-
Gregus, Gary, 1954-
Half Ice Drill Book

ISBN 1-890617-00-8

Editor: Chuck Menke
Layout: Dana Ausec
Preparation: Sarah Ross
Technical Advisor: Bob O'Connor

Printed by
Gowdy Printcraft
22 N. Sierra Madre
Colorado Springs, CO 80903